Olaf Stapledon

Twayne's English Authors Series

Kinley E. Roby, Editor

Northeastern University

OLAF STAPLEDON
Original illustration by
Laurence Donovan

Olaf Stapledon

By Patrick A. McCarthy

The University of Miami

Twayne Publishers · Boston

Olaf Stapledon

Patrick A. McCarthy

Copyright © 1982
Twayne Publishers
A Division of G. K. Hall & Company
70 Lincoln Street
Boston Massachusetts 02111

Library of Congress Cataloging in
Publication Data

McCarthy, Patrick A., 1945–
Olaf Stapledon.

(Twayne's English authors series:
TEAS 340)
Bibliography: pp. 158-62
Includes index.
1. Stapledon, Olaf, 1886–1950—
Criticism and interpretation.
2. Science fiction, English—History
and criticism.
I. Title.   II. Series.
PR6037.T18Z77 823'.912 81-6731
ISBN 0-8057-6826-2   AACR2

This one is for Kitty

Contents

About the Author

Patrick A. McCarthy was educated at the University of Virginia and the University of Wisconsin–Milwaukee. Since 1976 he has been at the University of Miami, where he teaches the science fiction course as well as classes in his major areas, modern British and Irish literature. He edits the *American Committee for Irish Studies Newsletter*, serves on the editorial board of *The Irish Renaissance Annual*, and contributes to a variety of scholarly journals. *The Riddles of Finnegans Wake*, his first book, was published in 1980 by Fairleigh Dickinson University Press.

Preface

This book is a critical introduction to the works of Olaf Stapledon, the most important British writer of science fiction since H. G. Wells. Following a chapter that outlines Stapledon's life and discusses briefly the major ideas that appear in the fiction, I have devoted five chapters to the analysis of theme and technique in each of Stapledon's published works (including the recently published short stories and the radio play). The final chapter assesses Stapledon's importance within, and his impact on, the field of science fiction.

There has been relatively little significant criticism of the works of Olaf Stapledon. Aside from John Kinnaird's monograph, soon to be published, the only extended study that attempts to cover the works in detail is a Canadian master's thesis by Roger Brunet. In the absence of a substantial body of criticism, I have enjoyed the luxury of developing my own reading of the works without always having to contend with the ideas of other critics. With this freedom comes a dual responsibility, not only to introduce general readers to the beauty and subtlety of Stapledon's art but also to lay a foundation for more specialized studies by later critics. Thus, I have been concerned with the broad outlines of Stapledon's thought, leaving to someone else the task of tracing in the works the influence of Spinoza or Hegel; I have indicated only the most important of the autobiographical elements in the fiction; and I have explored Stapledon's relationship to the handful of science fiction writers in whom his influence can be clearly detected, rather than undertaking a broader comparative study.

In the 1978 United Artists remake of *Invasion of the Body Snatchers,* the character played by Veronica Cartwright advises a customer at the Bellicec Mud Baths that Olaf Stapledon's *Star Maker* is "must reading." Long considered "must reading" by science fiction fans, Stapledon's novels also deserve to be studied by critics of the modern British novel, by anyone interested in the relationship of literature and philosophy, and by many other readers who would otherwise be reluctant to pick up a volume labeled "science fiction."

While I have tried to demonstrate Stapledon's importance as a writer of science fiction, the many references to such writers as Dante, Swift, Dostoevsky, and Camus are an indication that I have also read and evaluated his works in relation to the wider and more substantial tradition of European literature, and that I feel that his works deserve comparison with others that are certainly "must reading." Although it seems unlikely that the novels of Olaf Stapledon will ever be seen as part of the mainstream of modern literature, the books have a seriousness of purpose and an originality of conception that is found only in the works of the most important writers of any age. Today, thirty years after Stapledon's death, critics and general readers are beginning to discover the power of these strangely beautiful stories and to pay tribute to Stapledon's considerable skill as a literary artist. If my analysis of the works helps to open them to the wider audience they deserve, I shall have achieved my purpose in this study.

Patrick A. McCarthy

University of Miami

Acknowledgments

In writing this book I have incurred a great many debts, the most extensive of which I owe to Agnes Z. Stapledon and Harvey J. Satty. Mrs. Stapledon answered my endless questions with patience and good humor, both in our correspondence and during a long interview conducted at "Simon's Field." Harvey Satty, meanwhile, answered other questions and sent me many hard-to-get items, including some whose existence I did not suspect until they arrived in my mailbox. Like Mrs. Stapledon, Mr. Satty also read an early draft of each chapter and offered useful suggestions.

For help in obtaining primary and secondary materials I am indebted to Pat Pardo and the interlibrary loan staff at the University of Miami's Otto G. Richter Library; to Robert Crossley of the University of Massachusetts; and to Bruce Pelz, director of the Ephemera Division, Institute for Specialized Literature. I also want to thank the Research Council and the Arts and Humanities Committee of the University of Miami for granting me a Max Orovitz Summer Award to complete work on the book. Finally, I want to thank my colleague Laurence Donovan, who designed the illustration for the frontispiece.

I am grateful to Agnes Stapledon for permission to quote from all her husband's works; to Methuen & Co., Ltd., for permission to quote extensively from *Last and First Men, Last Men in London, Waking World, Odd John, Star Maker, A Man Divided,* and *The Opening of the Eyes;* to N. Frederick Nash, Rare Book Librarian at the University of Illinois at Urbana–Champaign, for permission to quote from a letter by Stapledon that is now part of the H. G. Wells Collection at Illinois; and to Penguin Books Ltd., for permission to quote two passages from the R. J. Hollingdale translation of Nietzsche's *Thus Spoke Zarathustra.*

Chronology

1886   William Olaf Stapledon, only child of William Clibbett Stapledon and Emmeline Miller Stapledon, born 10 May in Poolton cum Seacombe, the Wirral, England. Family spends next six years in Port Said, Egypt.

1894   Agnes Zena Miller, first of four children of Francis Edward Miller (brother of Emmeline Miller Stapledon) and Margaret Barnard Miller, born 25 May in New Zealand.

1905–1909 Stapledon attends Balliol College, Oxford, studying modern history (B.A., 1909).

1910–1911 Teaches at Manchester Grammar School and works in shipping offices in Liverpool and Port Said.

1912–1914 Lectures on history and literature under the auspices of the Worker's Educational Association (W.E.A.) and the University of Liverpool's extramural program. M.A., Balliol College, 1913. *Latter-Day Psalms* (poems) published 1914.

1915–1919 As a pacifist during World War I, serves in France and Belgium with the Friends' Ambulance Unit from July 1915 to January 1919. Marries Agnes Miller, 16 July 1919.

1920   Begins lecturing on industrial history, literature, philosophy, and psychology for the W.E.A. and the University Extension Board, University of Liverpool; continues lecturing for most of the remainder of his life. Stapledons move into home at 7 Grosvenor Avenue, West Kirby. 31 May, daughter, Mary Sydney, born.

1923   6 November, son, John David, born.

1925   Receives Ph.D. in philosophy from the University of Liverpool. Dissertation topic: "Meaning."

1926	Unsuccessful application for Lectureship in Moral Philosophy and in the History of Philosophy at the Queen's University of Belfast.
1929	*A Modern Theory of Ethics.*
1930	*Last and First Men;* composition of *Far Future Calling,* a radio play.
1932	*Last Men in London.* July, father dies.
1934	*Waking World.,*
1935	*Odd John.* Mother dies; Stapledon's inheritance is his primary source of income for the remainder of his life.
1936	20 April, first meeting with H. G. Wells.
1937	*Star Maker.*
1939	*Saints and Revolutionaries, New Hope for Britain,* and *Philosophy and Living.* March, Wolfgang Brueck, a Jewish refugee from Vienna, taken into the Stapledon home.
1940	Family moves to new home, Simon's Field, in Caldy.
1942	*Darkness and the Light* and *Beyond the "Isms."*
1944	*Old Man in New World* and *Sirius.* 14 December, John David Stapledon's ship, HMS *Aldenham,* is sunk by mine in the Adriatic, but Stapledon's son survives.
1946	*Death into Life* and *Youth and Tomorrow.* Speaks at a P.E.N. conference in Stockholm.
1947	*The Flames.*
1948	February and March, travels and lectures in France. August, attends the World Conference of Intellectuals for Peace in Wroclaw, Poland. October, presents paper on "Interplanetary Man?" at meeting of the British Interplanetary Society.
1949	March, travels to New York for The Cultural and Scientific Conference for Peace, a symposium sponsored by the National Council of the Arts, Sciences and Professions.
1950	*A Man Divided.* March, attends meeting of the Peace Aims Committee at Effinsward, Haywards Heath, Sussex; speaks on "Do the Ways to Peace Converge?" Dies 6 September, in Cheshire.

Chapter One

Preliminaries

The Early Years

Olaf Stapledon once claimed to have been "descended from a martyr who was killed for trying to educate people."[1] The claim is not quite accurate, for two reasons: first, because the presumed martyr-ancestor, Walter de Stapeldon, Bishop of Exeter, was murdered in 1326 by a Cheapside mob, not for his attempt to spread knowledge but in recognition of his services to the unpopular King Edward II; and second, because Olaf Stapledon was not descended from the Bishop but from his elder brother, Sir Richard de Stapeldon, co-founder (with the Bishop) of Stapeldon Hall, which is now known as Exeter College, Oxford. All questions of accuracy aside, however, the statement is interesting as an example of Stapledon's proud yet ironic attitude toward the family whose motto, *Mediocra firma*, he delighted in mistranslating as "a firm mediocrity." He had good reason to be proud of his family, even at a time when he felt generally rebellious against the cultural milieu that produced him, for his relatives were active, progressive, and successful. His father's much younger half-brother,[2] Sir Reginald George Stapledon (1882–1960), became an eminent botanist; the *Dictionary of National Biography* calls him the "pioneer of grassland science." Olaf Stapledon's grandfather, William Stapledon, founded a successful shipping agency that worked out of Port Said and Suez, Egypt; Olaf's father, William Clibbett Stapledon, managed the firm for many years before taking an important post with Alfred Holt and Co., a much larger shipping firm, in 1901. Over the years William Clibbett Stapledon became a prominent figure in English shipping, and in 1926, five years before his retirement, he was chairman of the Liverpool Steam Ship Owners' Association.

William Clibbett Stapledon and his wife, the former Emmeline Miller, were living in Port Said when she became pregnant, but Mrs.

Stapledon returned to England to give birth. On 10 May 1886 her only child, William Olaf Stapledon, was born in Poolton cum Seacombe, a suburb of Wallasey on the Wirral peninsula just south of Liverpool. The prosaic first name, William, was handed down from his father and grandfather and was quickly forgotten in order to distinguish the child from the other Williams in the family; the middle name, Olaf, was a more romantic choice, originating as it did in his mother's absorption in Norse literature during her pregnancy. Mrs. Stapledon and her baby returned to Port Said later in 1886, and Egypt remained their home until 1892, when Olaf and his mother moved back to England, partly because of the need to prepare for Olaf's education and partly because of Mrs. Stapledon's aversion to the hot, muggy Egyptian climate. For the next nine years Olaf saw his father only occasionally, until 1901 when his father's new position with the Blue Funnel Line of Alfred Holt and Co. reunited the family.

The details of those early years in Egypt and England have never been thoroughly explored, although it is known that Olaf was particularly fond of a small terrier named Rip. But Stapledon's later statements leave no doubt that he was devoted to his father, an open-minded and understanding man who stimulated his son's imagination and set an example of mildly individualistic and unconventional behavior. On the other hand, Olaf's mother was more concerned with proprieties than her husband. In *Youth and Tomorrow*, Stapledon was to recall his mother's intrusion into one of his father's science lessons, and her insistence that there were some "sacred mysteries of life"—in this case, the contents of a fertilized bird's egg—that ought to be kept secret from children.[3] In the same book, Stapledon remembered his mother's household as the very picture of late Victorian conventionality:

My mother, like all her friends, had a "day," and her cards bore the legend "At Home, first and third Tuesdays," or whatever day she had chosen. . . . As a child in Egypt and a boy in England, I sometimes had to be present on these occasions, washed, and in a stiff Eton collar. I handed round the cakes and cups of tea, and sat in the least comfortable chair.[4]

Despite her generally conventional manner, Olaf's mother was surprisingly advanced in certain ways. As a Unitarian, she believed in freedom of religious thought; and since her husband seems to have been completely nonreligious, Olaf grew up without any strong religious beliefs and developed into an agnostic. Mrs. Stapledon's enthusiasm for the works of the great English critic John Ruskin seems also to have been a major influence on the development of her son's mind: Sam Moskowitz credits Ruskin's writings with inculcating in Olaf a profound sympathy for socialist causes.[5] In any case, the Stapledon household was one where ideas of all kinds could be discussed openly and where free thinking was not only tolerated but encouraged.

Stapledon's early education took place at a local dame-school, at the Liverpool College Upper School, and eventually at the Abbotsholme School, a progressive boarding school. In 1905 he entered Oxford University—not Exeter College, as one might expect of a descendant of its founder, but Balliol College. There, he read modern history and, at nine stone ten pounds (136 lbs.—approximately his weight for the remainder of his life), he was the lightest man on the Balliol rowing team. Following his graduation in 1909, Stapledon worked for his father's firm, first in Liverpool and later in Port Said, and he taught for a year at the Manchester Grammar School. Neither job suited him very well: at the shipping office, according to his own account, he managed to lose twenty pounds in petty cash, and at the school the history plays that his students acted out brought complaints from other teachers that altogether too much noise was emanating from his classroom. If the character of Paul in *Last Men in London* is to be taken as autobiographical in this respect, Stapledon may also have felt uncertain of his authority as a schoolmaster and may have doubted his competence to handle the post.

In 1912, however, he entered into work more suited to his talents when he began delivering lectures for the Worker's Educational Association (W.E.A.) and also began lecturing extramurally for the University of Liverpool. This occupation, which he was to pass on to Victor Smith in his late novel, *A Man Divided,* was especially welcome since it provided him with a forum for expounding his socialist interpretation of industrial history. Meanwhile, he took an M.A. in history at Balliol College in 1913. The following year, however, the advent of World War I put a temporary halt to Stapledon's career as lecturer. His experiences in the conflict insured that he would continue to be a socialist and pacifist in revolt against the system that had produced him.

Latter-Day Psalms and World War I

That Stapledon held his unconventional leftist views before the war might be difficult to prove if it were not for the appearance in 1914 of a slender volume of his poems, *Latter-Day Psalms*.[6] The poems, written in a sort of free verse with a form and diction that attempt to imitate biblical psalms, are not particularly distinguished, and it was known that their publication was subsidised by Stapledon's generous and indulgent father. What is interesting about the psalms is their introduction of several themes and attitudes that Stapledon was to develop in a more sophisticated fashion in his fictional and philosophical writings.

A variety of voices speak throughout the twenty-four poems of the collection, but most often the speaker is Stapledon in his role of the skeptic who constantly searches for values beyond those affirmed by everyday experience. In the first psalm, "The City," Stapledon enters the City of Man to look for evidence of God's benevolence in men's lives. Finding only poverty, hatred, and spiritual stagnation, he turns from God in horror:

I said in my pride, "If there be God, he shall be no God of mine. I will go
   my way, and live according as my soul wills.
I will make war upon thee, evil God. Though thou slay me, I will contrive
   justice and mercy against thy will."

The following poems trace a spiritual journey from this simple rejection of the world as he finds it to a more complex and ambiguous affirmation of transcendent spiritual verities. A tentative move toward the latter position can be seen in the second poem, "Spirit," where the city lights mirror the "multitude of stars" that seem to declare the excellence of the spirit that speaks in the poet's heart. The speaker, however, errs in his assumption that the transcendent spirit is God, for in "Humanity" the Soul of All Men speaks within him, saying that it is not God but is instead an evolving spirit yearning toward union with

God and born partly out of the sufferings of individual people. Thus enlightenment or spiritual beauty may be the product of spiritual torment.

Most of the psalms deal with Stapledon's perception of the nature and purpose of the spiritual reality that he senses throughout the universe. In "God," he raises two ideas that are investigated more thoroughly in *Star Maker* and other later works: the possibilities that the spirit may continue to live after the end of the physical universe and that there may be further universes. In a series of eight poems toward the end of the volume he adapts classical, Christian, and Hindu terms to explore various aspects of the spirit and of God: Athena, for example, is the indwelling spirit of beauty, nobility, and wisdom in mankind, while Satan is depicted much as William Blake saw him, as the principle of unrestrained creative energy in rebellion against God in his role as divine judge and lawmaker. The series of metaphysical poems concludes with "Christ" and "Brahma," both of which celebrate the transcendence of man's individuality and the immersion of the awakened soul of man (Christ) within the spirit of the cosmos (Brahma).

One of the most interesting of the poems is "Men," which contrasts two aspects of individual human beings: their customary selfish mood, which reflects the shallow values of their age, and an occasional second mood in which they suddenly become aware of a higher value or reality that can redeem their lives. Men "trample on their kindred for a little bread; yet for a vision they forget themselves." The idea that we must "forget ourselves" is restated in "Salvation," a poem that denounces the self-seeking turn toward God that is motivated by the desire to save one's individual soul:

Men, yea, and the stars, call upon thee for help. But thou broodest on thy soul.
If indeed thou hast a soul, forget it. Come out from it, and enter into the hope and fear that is greater than thou.
Sacrifice even thy soul gladly if the world need. Or, if thou canst save it, save it not to be thine, but to be God's.

Other poems reflect more directly Stapledon's concern with contemporary social problems. In "My Cup Runneth Over," he asks why he should be so fortunate in his perception of spiritual beauty while others remain blind, largely because of the poverty that blights their whole lives. "Have I stolen my brother's blessings?" he asks, and self-consciously dedicates himself to uplifting the working class, presumably through lecturing for the W.E.A. Revolutionary voices of the working class speak in the next two poems, "The Rebel" and "Labour," rejecting the conventional image of God which they regard as·an aspect of their oppressive circumstances. The two poems most imme-diately relevant to the world situation in 1914 are the final entries in *Latter-Day Psalms*, "War" and "Peace," which may have been composed after the outbreak of the war. In "War," the martial spirit of the combatants on both sides speaks as a kind of perversion of religious faith, urging the young into battle against an enemy that it envisions as an agent of the devil. In the mistaken belief that they are fighting a holy war, the combatants actually rise above the limitations of their selfhoods, but their mistaken understanding of the nature of the war guarantees that there will be no true spiritual awakening as a result of this adventure, only slaughter. The ironic final poem, "Peace," however, provides an ambiguous conclusion for the volume in its suggestion that the war may lead to an advancement of the spirit or it may simply lead to needless death:

And the souls of the dead shall be gathered into the spirit; and the spirit shall flourish.
There shall be a new heaven and a new earth, and joy shall be again. But the dead shall not come back.

Some insight into *Latter-Day Psalms* may be gained from its title and epigraph, both of which point to Thomas Carlyle's *Latter-Day Pamphlets* (1850). On the surface, Stapledon might appear to have little in common with Carlyle, a reactionary whose ultraconservative views of society placed him at the other extreme of the political spectrum; yet both men were motivated by a sense of the spiritual bankruptcy of their times, and if their reactions to the problem differed, that difference was probably less important than their common perception of the problem. Both saw that the present social order was moribund; both rejected simple religious fundamentalism and its antithesis, rationalism, as solutions to man's spiritual crisis. And as the World War came ever closer, Carlyle's prophetic words cited in Stapledon's epigraph must have seemed to Stapledon increasingly appropriate:

There must be a new world if there is to be any world at all! . . . These days of universal death must be days of universal new birth, if the ruin is not to be total and final! It is a Time to make the dullest man consider; and ask himself, Whence *he* came? Whither he is bound?—A veritable 'New Era,' to the foolish as well as to the wise.

Throughout the summer of 1914, the idea that the "days of universal death" might lead to "universal new birth" was one way of coping with the disaster that Europeans found themselves unable to avoid, but the ambiguous conclusion of *Latter-Day Psalms* demonstrates that Stapledon was not altogether convinced that a new world was just around the corner.

At the onset of the war Stapledon, like many other young men with left-wing inclinations, found himself beset with doubts about the war. Years later, in *Last Men in London,* he analyzed the attitudes toward the war among five main groups of people.[7] First there were those who saw the war in purely personal terms, either as a source of profit or as a danger to their lives. Next were the martial romantics, those who accepted war, the "martial code," and the "hero ideal" as expressive of man's highest values and saw war as an opportunity for individual men to rise above themselves. (It is the voice of these people that speaks most loudly in the poem "War.") A more common type, however, was the person who knew in his heart that the war was wrong but suppressed his doubts through sophistic arguments and the illusion that the enemy was an ogre. A fourth group included those people who were dismayed by the war and by the romantic image of the warrior-knight, but who in the end supported the war because of loyalty to their countrymen and because of their belief that a victory by the enemy would lead to tyranny, while a victory by their side might lead to Carlyle's "universal new birth." The last group, the only one to oppose the war, was composed of the pacifists; and among the pacifists were some who, like Stapledon and his fictional equivalent,

Paul, entered into noncombatant service in order "to accept so far as possible on the one hand the great common agony, and on the other the private loneliness of those who cannot share the deepest passions of their fellows." In this state of mind, Olaf Stapledon joined the ambulance corps of the Society of Friends.

In an article written twenty years later, Stapledon described quite candidly the welter of conflicting emotions that dictated his course during the war.[8] Not an absolute pacifist, he nevertheless believed that modern war was "likely to undermine civilisation" through its combinations of "nationalism . . . and militarism, and the glib surrender of one's moral responsibility to an authority that was not really fit to bear it." His decision to join the Friends' Ambulance Unit, in which he served as a driver in France and Belgium, was the product of "two overmastering and wholesome impulses, the will to share in the common ordeal and the will to make some kind of protest against the common folly." Throughout the war years Stapledon was uncomfortable with his quasi-military position: he worried that the French might think him *un embusqué* ("a shirker"), and he was secretly delighted to be awarded the Croix de Guerre, but in later years he was embarrassed enough by military decorations that few people knew he had received not only the Croix but also the 1914/1915 Star Riband and the Victory Riband. On the other hand, he never regretted having worked as an ambulance driver in S.S.A. 13 (*Section Sanitaire Anglaise Treize*): if the path he chose was an uneasy compromise between genuine militarism and total pacifism, it was still the only course consistent with his desire to serve the human spirit. In the last thirty years of his life, that same desire motivated him in his careers as public lecturer, philosophical writer, and novelist.

Private and Public Life

In 1919, six months after his discharge from the ambulance unit, Stapledon married his twenty-five year old Australian cousin, Agnes Zena Miller. They began the business of having a family almost at once: the following May, Agnes Stapledon gave birth to their first child, Mary Sydney (her middle name reflects her mother's Australian upbringing), and a son, John David, was born in 1923. Before the birth of Mary Sydney, the Stapledons settled in their new house at 7 Grosvenor Avenue in West Kirby, a mile or two from Caldy, where Stapledon's parents lived. This house was to be Stapledon's residence for the next two decades, and it was there that he wrote several of the science fiction novels on which his reputation now depends: the future history *Last and First Men* and its sequel, *Last Men in London;* his superman novel, *Odd John;* and his cosmic masterpiece of insight and discovery, *Star Maker.*

While Stapledon's novels and other writings are evidence of a remarkably original and unconventional mind, his personal life appears to have been somewhat more commonplace. His family had always led a robust outdoor life, and Olaf was an avid walker, mountain climber, swimmer (in all seasons), and tennis player. He was devoted to his children, fashioning model boats and making up stories for them, and he tried to stimulate their imaginations and to foster creativity and originality in both of them. (Thus, after a trip to the west of Ireland, he encouraged his son's expressed desire to build a curragh.) Such a happy and stable family life appears to have been important to Stapledon in two ways that concern his writing. First, Stapledon needed the familiarity and solidity of a middle-class home life as a counterweight to the turbulence of his imaginative work. After writing all day about alien intelligences or a superhuman mind or a war that nearly destroys the human race, it must have been a relief for Stapledon to put all that aside and absorb himself in the everyday affairs of his wife and children. More important, however, was Stapledon's vision of the family as his primary model of community and his insistence that the only true spiritual growth begins with the development of "personality-in-community," the growth of the individual person as a result of his involvement with other members of his community. Rejecting both the Western ideal of "individualism," which he saw as largely an excuse for capitalistic exploitation of others, and the communistic suppression of the individual in favor of the group, Stapledon sought instead a social or political unit that would encourage the growth of true individuality. In politics, such an ideal implied a variety of democratic socialism; in the imaginative vision of his works, it took many forms including the "sexual groups" of *Last and First Men* and the colony of supernormals in *Odd John;* but in his personal life, the most important group for the enhancement of personality-in-community was the family.

Like many of his characters, Stapledon was a late developer: at the age of thirty-three he found himself newly married and undecided about what career he wanted to pursue. He returned to lecturing for the W.E.A. and the University of Liverpool Extension Board, but his lectures (or "talks," as he preferred to call them) never netted him enough money to support his family, so his father regularly gave him money to supplement his income. Much of this money came from family investments, and true to his socialist principles, Stapledon felt self-conscious about living off "dividends and other ill-gotten gains";[9] but he also realized that the full development of his abilities required more time than he would find if he were to have to earn a living through his labor. The financial support became particularly important when Stapledon decided to continue his education by enrolling in the graduate program at the University of Liverpool, where he read psychology and philosophy. In 1925 he received a doctorate in philosophy, but the degree did not lead to a regular appointment as a university lecturer. On his fortieth birthday, in 1926, Stapledon had still not determined what he wanted to do with his life, although he was reasonably certain that he wanted to propagate his ideas to a wider audience than his extramural lectureship gave him.

Several courses were open to him, and Stapledon took them all. The first course was involvement in political and social action groups. Over the last quarter century of his life Stapledon became associated with many such groups, including the Federation of Progressive Societies and Individuals, the League of Nations Union, Cosmopolis,[10] the Progressive League, the Association for Education in Cititzenship, Richard Acland's Common Wealth Party, and the 1941 Committee. He also belonged to P.E.N., the international writers' association, as well as the British Interplanetary Society. Involvement in so many groups entailed a certain amount of lecturing—mostly in England, but also at a P.E.N meeting in Stockholm, at meetings of various organizations in post–World War II France, and at the World Conference of Intellectuals for Peace in Wroclaw, Poland. Stapledon's only trip to America, to attend a peace conference in New York in

March 1949, gave him a certain notoriety: the conference was sponsored by the leftist National Council of the Arts, Sciences and Professions, and when the American government refused visas to the other British delegates Stapledon, an alternate delegate, came alone. Stapledon's hopes for world peace were not enhanced by the conference and its reception, which included an inflammatory article in *Life* that was almost as one-sidedly opposed to the conference as most of the members of the conference were one-sidedly anti-American;[11] returning to England, Stapledon worried that war might break out "at any moment."[12]

Partly through his writings and partly through his association with political or educational groups, Stapledon developed an extensive correspondence with well-known literary, philosophical, and political figures of his day. Among the many letters left in Stapledon's library at "Simon's Field," the home where he and his family moved in 1940, is a file marked "Special correspondence," which contains letters from fifty people including J. B. S. Haldane, Julian Huxley, Philip Toynbee, John Middleton Murry, Harold Laski, John Strachey, J. D. Beresford, Gerald Heard, Aldous Huxley, C. E. M. Joad, and Bertrand Russell. Letters from H. G. Wells are also in the file, and the Wells Collection at the University of Illinois includes over two dozen letters that Stapledon wrote to Wells between 1931 and 1942. Some of the letters to Wells are brief social notes about luncheon dates or acknowledgments that Stapledon received a book that Wells sent, but others are requests that Wells sign a petition or speak before a local group, and in several letters Stapledon takes issue with Wells's ideas or tries to clarify or expound on his own thoughts. Even though his natural shyness and the fact that he lived in a somewhat remote corner of England prevented Stapledon from developing intimate personal relationships with people like Wells, his correspondence and travel enabled him to play a minor but active role in the debate over social and philosophical issues in England.

It was his writings, however, that Stapledon considered the most effective agent for the propagation of his ideas. After publishing a series of philosophical essays in the late twenties, he tried to make his mark as a philosopher with a highly technical (and largely ignored) volume, *A Modern Theory of Ethics* (1929). Stapledon's nonfiction

works were never to attract the devoted readership that anxiously
awaited the publication of his novels, but throughout most of the rest
of his life he alternated between the more successful, and certainly
more popular, imaginative works and a series of books and articles
that outlined his views of man, society, and the cosmos.

Those views, which reappear in the fiction, are based on several
premises. First, while he is skeptical about orthodox religions and
eschews all systems of belief that aim primarily at the salvation of individual souls, Stapledon is convinced that those who see man in purely
material or biological terms—communists, advocates of certain psychological theories, and H. G. Wells, for example—are equally, although
perhaps more understandably, misguided. Instead, Stapledon argues
that the "painful rediscovery and restatement of 'spiritual values' [is]
the most important feature of our time."[13] By "spiritual values" he
means those values that are based on our awareness of ourselves in
relation to other selves and to the universe; and since that awareness is
constantly evolving—or *should* evolve—as man deepens in awareness
and develops social institutions that promote the advancement of spirit
in all people, it follows that the values to which man ought to give
allegiance are not immutable but must evolve in accordance with
"man's rapidly changing conditions."[14] The most "awakened" or "developed" attitude, then, expresses itself in a mood of objective detach-
ment from parochial or individual concerns. Intelligence, Stapledon
contends, may appear in a variety of forms, including nonhuman or extraterrestrial forms of life, and we would do well to try to establish
contact with other types of intelligence. Ultimately, Stapledon argues,
we should view our world and ourselves from a "cosmic" point of
view, a view based on concrete experience of ourselves and others but
capable of transcending all merely human values if they fail to support
even higher values.

The source of those higher values is not clear, largely because
Stapledon consistently maintains an agnostic attitude toward the
existence of a deity or ruling spirit in the cosmos. Unwilling to commit
himself without better evidence, he refers in several of his books to a
godlike figure, but always leaves his readers the option of regarding
this ruling spirit simply as a metaphor for the idealized form of the
"cosmic spirit," the evolving spirit of the sentient universe itself. Nor

is it ever certain that the spiritual values that Stapledon advocates—love, for example—are sanctioned by the god or Star Maker, although Stapledon argues that the development follows the plan of the cosmic creator.

On the other hand, Stapledon is more confident about the problem of man's immediate existence. Twentieth-century man, he contends, faces a crisis in his spiritual development that could determine whether man evolves into a more mentally and spiritually aware being or slides back into bestiality. Modern man is caught between two moods, or wills, or sets of values: a lower, "archaic," mood in which man wants to dominate others, and a higher, fully human, mood in which the will to dominate is replaced by an awareness of others as distinct from ourselves yet important to our own development. In political terms, the first mood manifests itself in "tribalism"—nationalism, totalitarianism, and reversion to what Stapledon terms the "herd-mentality"— while man's "developed values are those which centre round the remote but increasingly important ideal of a world-community of very diverse but mutually respecting and mutually enriching individuals."[15] In some ways, all of Stapledon's books, fiction and nonfiction alike, may be said to derive from a concern with this crisis, this struggle between two competing wills. Moreover, in Stapledon's view the political struggles of his day, including the Spanish Civil War and World War II, mirrored the battle of these two wills in the hearts of individual men, so that all political choices are fundamentally "religious."[16] The corollary to this observation is that the spiritual development of individual people cannot continue far without corresponding social reforms, and that political changes that improve man's material conditions without awakening people to higher spiritual values will at best be temporary.

Although they are based on long years of reading and reflection, the major ideas that Stapledon develops in most of the books are accessible to virtually all common readers. The general clarity and the logical organization of books like *Waking World, Saints and Revolutionaries, New Hope for Britain,* and *Youth and Tomorrow* are the product of many years' experience in simplifying complex ideas for lectures for the W.E.A. On the other hand, the upper limits of Stapledon's vision are often vague—necessarily so, since he was constantly reaching after ideas that man, in his present state of development, can understand only obscurely. When he turned to fiction, however, Stapledon sensed that he could convert his problem into an asset by abandoning "mainstream" literary forms and experimenting with situations and narrative styles that allowed him to give concrete form to his philosophical speculations. The result of that experiment was one of the most important bodies of work yet produced by a writer of science fiction.

Choosing a Form: Stapledon and Science Fiction

In 1930, when Olaf Stapledon published *Last and First Men,* he began a twenty-year career as a major writer in a genre that he knew little about. For the most part, as Walter H. Gillings discovered when he interviewed "the philosopher of fantasy" seven years later, Stapledon's works owed little to those of other science fiction writers. "I am afraid I do not approach the subject [of science fiction] from quite the same standpoint that you do," Stapledon told Gillings; "I am more interested in philosophy. . . . In my fiction, I am only concerned with fantastic imaginings in so far as they seem to have a more or less philosophical bearing on the subject." Although he admitted that he had read some works by Jules Verne, Edgar Rice Burroughs, and of course H. G. Wells, he noted that he had seen his first science fiction magazine in 1936, and had been both surprised that so many science fiction stories were being published, and appalled that they were generally so badly written.[17] Indeed, at the time he wrote *Last and First Men,* Stapledon may not have heard the term "science fiction," which had recently been invented by Hugo Gernsback as an alternative to the clumsy term "scientifiction," another Gernsbackian coinage. Instead, Stapledon preferred to think of his works as examples of "philosophical fiction"—or, to cite the phrase he used in his first letter to Wells, "scientific romances."[18]

That letter is particularly important since it shows Stapledon trying to establish his independence from Wells even as he notes the profound influence Wells has had on his work. On the one hand he apologizes for not acknowledging his "huge debt" to Wells in the introduction to *Last and First Men;* his defense, he says, is that "A man does not record his debt to the air he breathes in common with everyone else." On the other hand, he is careful to observe that he has read only two of Wells's scientific fictions: a novel, *The War of the Worlds* (1898), and a short story, "The Star" (1899). It is a little surprising that Stapledon wrote science fiction novels without having encountered such classics as *The Time Machine, The Island of Dr. Moreau,* and *The First Men in the Moon,* where Wells experiments with themes that Stapledon was to treat in his own books. Of course, the same ideas are developed in many of Wells's books of social philosophy, and Wells's most popular book, *The Outline of History,* undoubtedly suggested to Stapledon the possibility of writing a fictional history of man's future in his own first novel.

Despite his meager knowledge of Wells's science fiction, however, Stapledon must have known that within the field of science fiction, Wells, along with other futuristic writers like Yevgeny Zamiatin (*We,* 1920) and Edward Bellamy (*Looking Backward,* 1888), used speculative stories as vehicles for the discussion of the relationship among man's culture, psychology, and technology. This branch of science fiction may be traced to Mary Shelley's *Frankenstein* (1818), which, despite its Gothic aura, is fundamentally a serious examination of the scientist as Promethean figure. Indeed, the roots of the type of science fiction associated with Wells and Stapledon—and later with Aldous Huxley, George Orwell, Arthur C. Clarke, Stanislaw Lem, Anthony Burgess, Kurt Vonnegut, and others—may be traced to Swiftian satire. The competing branch of science fiction, which began with the fantasies of Edgar Rice Burroughs and became associated in the 1930s with the wild space operas of E. E. "Doc" Smith, must have seemed to Stapledon to have little to do with his writings, or those of Wells. Largely a product of the American pulp tradition, this brand of escapist science fiction had little, if any, influence on Stapledon and other British writers.

Like most serious writers of science fiction in the years before World War II, Stapledon based much of his vision of science on several ideas that first appeared in the nineteenth century. Patrick Parrinder has noted that man's faith in scientific and technological "progress" was opposed by "the Darwinian theory of evolution, with its implication that the biological constitution of man was open to perpetual change and instability, and the Second Law of Thermody-

namics which posited an irreversible process of entropy, or what
became known as the 'running-down universe.' "[19] It is doubtful,
however, that any writer has ever taken more seriously than Stapledon
the conditions laid down by this scientific world view. First, Stapledon
could see that man's evolution could lead upward or downward; that
"evolution" could imply spiritual development as well as biological
change; and that biological and spiritual evolution are closely related
to each other. Thus in one book after another he envisions various
types of genetic engineering aimed at creating a higher form of an
intelligent species. Moreover, the fact that the physical universe is
inexorably subject to entropy lends increased urgency to the spiritual
quest that is at the heart of much of Stapledon's fiction. Finally,
Stapledon's training as a philosopher and his emphasis on broad cosmic
themes rather than on the development of plot insured that he would
treat these scientific themes and examine their implications more
directly than any other writer of science fiction.

   Stapledon has always been an anomalous figure within his own
field. The scope of his works is what truly sets him apart: in his books
thousands, millions, even billions of years can pass, whole races can
rise to a highly civilized stage and disappear, galaxies can be
obliterated. Meanwhile, the reader is asked to consider the relevance
of all this to modern man. Occasionally criticized for their lack of
"narrative drive" and "human interest," more often neglected because
of the demands they place on their readers, Stapledon's books are all
too often viewed simply as philosophical treatises masked by a thin veil
of fictional narration. The charge is not altogether false, for to
Stapledon the ideas in his novels are all-important, the narrative line
serving primarily as an imaginative device to provoke confrontation
with the philosophical argument. Of course in theory, the same may
be said of other writers, but in practice such an extreme emphasis on
the ideas of a novel is unknown among other science fiction writers:
even novels like *The Time Machine* and *A Clockwork Orange* can
probably be read strictly as adventure fiction, although Wells and
Burgess would undoubtedly consider such a reading inadequate.[20]
With Stapledon's books, however, there is no way of avoiding the
argument short of closing the book and forgetting about it. But this is
not to say that the novels lack aesthetic interest, for in their

conception—and even occasionally in their narrative development—
they are among the most original and stimulating works in modern
literature. Thus in the chapters that follow, I shall consider both the
literary merits and the political, social, and metaphysical implications
of Stapledon's fiction, beginning with the novel whose unexpected
popularity convinced Stapledon to continue writing. That novel was
Last and First Men.

Chapter Two

The Myth of Man

Shaping Things to Come

Olaf Stapledon once said that the "general plan" of his first novel, *Last and First Men* (1930), "came to me in a flash as I was watching seals from the cliffs of Anglesea."[1] The themes of the book, however, had been germinating in his mind for some time. A concise introduction to some of those themes may be obtained from J. B. S. Haldane's essays "Man's Destiny" and "The Last Judgment,"[2] which appeared a few years before *Last and First Men*. In "Man's Destiny," Haldane discusses possible futures for mankind. We could be wiped out by some apocalyptic disaster such as a war, plague, or astronomical catastrophe, but on the whole Haldane suspects that man and his civilization are unlikely to be destroyed so dramatically. On the other hand, man can evolve toward a higher state of civilization or degenerate into a barbaric species, depending on how he uses knowledge gained through scientific research. Haldane feels that the latter possibility is the more probable of the two:

It is quite likely that, after a golden age of happiness and peace, during which all the immediately available benefits of science will be realized, mankind will very gradually deteriorate. Genius will become ever rarer, our bodies a little weaker in each generation; culture will slowly decline, and in a few thousand or a few hundred thousand years—it does not much matter which—mankind will return to barbarism, and finally become extinct.[3]

On the other hand, if we use scientific knowledge to further our evolution, the possibilities are staggering. Men and women of the future could enjoy perfect health and an intellectual and cultural life far beyond what we can presently conceive; man's life could last thousands of years, each minute "lived with all the passion of a lover or a discoverer." Eventually, Haldane suggests, man will expand his horizons even further, through interplanetary and then through interstellar travel. It is possible, he says, that man's "intellectual and spiritual progress" will be limitless. But—to restate his thesis—the choice whether to evolve upward or downward rests with us, for "unless he can control his own evolution as he is learning to control that of his domestic plants and animals, man and all his works will go down into oblivion and darkness."

Haldane deals with similar issues in "The Last Judgment," an essay which Sam Moskowitz credits with having inspired the "design" of *Last and First Men*.[4] Haldane imagines a future in which the use of tidal power affects the Earth's rotation and eventually causes the moon to disintegrate and fall upon the Earth. Long before the end of the world, the human race migrates to Venus, having first remade itself to fit the conditions it would face in the hostile Venerian environment. Not at all chastised by the ill effects of its technology, mankind plans to return to Earth in another thirty-five thousand years, when the planet is once again inhabitable; future possibilities include the colonization of the rest of the solar system and even the spread of human life to other solar systems and other galaxies. Again, Haldane's point is that to a large extent we can control our destinies: "If humanity can enlarge the scope of its will as it has enlarged the reach of its intellect, it will escape [its] end. If not, the judgment will have gone out against it, and man and all his works will perish eternally."[5]

Last and First Men was Stapledon's initial attempt to use science fiction to deal with questions posed by Haldane and other critics of science and modern society. The project may have begun simply as an experiment; certainly Stapledon never expected the book to be as popular, both with critics and with ordinary readers, as it was. In any case, however, the critical success of *Last and First Men,* which established Stapledon as heir to the mantle of H. G. Wells, confirmed Stapledon's belief that fantastic fiction was a suitable medium for his ideas.

The Shape of the Thing

Having decided to write a future history on the model of "The Last Judgment," Stapledon was faced with the problem of point of view:

how should the story be told? The author of *Last and First Men* had several avenues open to him. For example, he could have had a modern man travel into the future, like Wells's Time Traveller, stop at different points to see how the world will be getting on, and return to our era to report to us. Or he could have reversed the Wellsian pattern by having a man from the future visit the twentieth century to tell modern man about the coming millenia. A third possibility was to have someone fall into a trance and have a vision of the future, like the vision of God achieved by Mr. Vankirk in Edgar Allan Poe's "Mesmeric Revelation." Or he could have fictionalized his audience by setting the narration of the story well in the future and pretending that the novel is, say, a history text or a series of lectures for the history students of a time millions of years from now.

Stapledon avoided these and other obvious solutions by having his novel narrated to us by one of the Eighteenth (Last) Men, a superrace living on Neptune two billion years hence. The Last Men have discovered how to explore the past mentally, by entering into the minds of beings who, having once existed, continue to exist in the realm of eternal time. Not only that, but the Last Men can communicate with these past beings much as a radio broadcaster can speak to people in distant places. From our perspective, then, the book consists of a future history, while from the narrator's point of view it is a description of past events. Moreover, although the Neptunian narrator insists that he is the true author of the book and that Stapledon is just his amanuensis, he admits that Stapledon "thinks he is merely contriving a work of fiction" and "neither believes [his story] himself, nor expects others to believe it" (13).[6] Thus the narrator's attitude toward his work is inherently ironic, like that of a prophet who knows that his predictions will not be recognized as the truth. The point of view of the novel is also ironic because the narrator knows so much more than we can hope to grasp that for all practical purposes he can be regarded as an omniscient narrator who speaks with absolute and irrefutable authority; yet he is also a particular human (or superhuman) being. In choosing this person to narrate his story, Stapledon allowed himself the advantages of the omniscient narrator's detached, objective posture while retaining the more clearly individualized perspective of the first person narrator, the eye-witness who is himself part of his story.

The details of that story are too numerous to review here, but a brief outline will convey some idea of the scope of the book. Stapledon's narrator describes the histories of five species of men on Earth, three on Venus, and ten on Neptune. We belong to the first phase of the First Men, a race that suffers from nationalism, from the inability of man's animal nature to cope with the demands of the world as a social community, and from the combination of technical genius with man's social, moral, and aesthetic immaturity. After a series of nationalistic wars, man founds a World State, but germ warfare used by the government against its own workers devastates much of the planet and leads to a dark age that endures for a hundred thousand years. A second great civilization of the First Men emerges in Patagonia, but in time a nuclear disaster nearly destroys the race. Only thirty-five people survive, and their colony in Siberia is further reduced when a quarrel within the group causes some of the survivors to migrate to Labrador, where they descend to a subhuman state.

The Second Men, who descend from the Siberian colony, build a great civilization but manage to destroy their culture—and nearly annihilate the entire race—when they use germ warfare against Martian invaders. Their descendants, the Third Men, are experts at genetic engineering; they produce an artificial race, the Fourth Men or Great Brains, who in turn create a new species, the Fifth Men. This race of superior beings creates an advanced culture but is forced to migrate to Venus when its scientists learn that the moon will disintegrate and its pieces will crash on the Earth. On Venus, physical mutations caused by the new environment produce the Sixth Men. Fascinated with flight, the Sixth Men create a race of flying beings, the Seventh Men; but in time the flyers are overthrown by "crippled" (nonflying) members of their species. Threatened with a flightless existence, the flyers commit suicide. Once again mankind remakes itself, this time creating a "strictly pedestrian" species, the Eighth Men, whose technological genius turns Venus into "an engineer's paradise." But when the Eighth Men discover that "a volume of non-luminous gas" will enter the solar system and cause an explosion of the sun, they are again forced to migrate—this time to Neptune.

The first Neptunian race, the Ninth Men, devolves into various subhuman species, but hundreds of millions of years later, after a variety of transitional species have come and gone, the Fourteenth

Men emerge and explore their planet. Natural evolution produces the Fifteenth Men, who decide to create a higher species in which there will be no "disease, suffocating toil, senility, misunderstanding, ill-will" (270). The Sixteenth Men, in turn, create the Seventeenth, and they construct still another species, the Eighteenth, or Last, Men. These great beings are especially interesting because of two aspects of their culture: the "sexual group" and the "racial experience." In the first, sexual activity is used to bring members of the group together, and the experiences of each person enrich every member of the group. Periods of mental communion with the entire group produce a group-mind in which all members are able to participate in the minds and bodies of the others and the sexual group rises to a new level of awareness. In the racial experience, the pattern of the sexual group is carried out on a broader scale: the entire world becomes one, but individuals do not lose their identities. In this awakened state, the racial mind is able to apprehend clearly "the true nature of space and time, mind and its objects, cosmical striving and cosmical perfection."

Despite the high state of their civilization, the Last Men are a doomed species, for a "mad star" infected by "a fantastic acceleration of its vital process" will cause our sun to disintegrate rapidly and to destroy all life in the solar system. In an Epilogue, narrated 20,000 years after the rest of the book, changes in the sun have already led to a decline in the Last Men. The racial mind cannot be revived, and the sexual groups are disintegrating; moreover, they are unable to recall the insights they achieved through their earlier experiences. But the last of the Last Men, the youngest and most highly developed, provides the conclusion through his declaration that even though the universe is indifferent to us, man is "eternally a beauty in the eternal form of things" and "It is very good to have been man."

Last and First Men: Some Major Themes

At first glance, what is most startling about *Last and First Men* is its scope: even within a genre that often stretches the boundaries of space and time far beyond what one might expect in a realistic novel, a chronology of two billion years is highly unusual. Stapledon makes the most of the broad dimensions of his narrative. In the introduction he hints at the thematic importance of the scale of his book when he asks us to "brood upon these magnitudes, to draw out the mind toward them, to feel the littleness of [our] here and now, and of the moment of civilization which [we] call history" (14). He returns to this idea in his opening chapter:

Long before the human spirit awoke to clear cognizance of the world and itself, it sometimes stirred in its sleep, opened bewildered eyes, and slept again. One of these moments of precocious experience embraces the whole struggle of the First Men from savagery towards civilization. Within that moment, you stand almost in the very instant when the species attains its zenith. Scarcely at all beyond your own day is this early culture to be seen progressing, and already in your time the mentality of the race shows signs of decline. (19)

Thus, when measured against the immensity of man's experience—an experience which at the end of the novel will be termed "this brief music that is man" as Stapledon shifts scales and measures man's two billion year saga against the far greater history of the cosmos—our own age seems remarkably fleeting. (Our sense of the brevity of human history is increased by a series of time scales, the last of which reduces to a dot the whole period from the formation of the planets down to the end of man.) This introductory passage also demonstrates Stapledon's tendency to treat mankind mythically, dealing with the history of the human race as if it were the life of an individual man. Here, Stapledon's metaphoric description of man is reminiscent of William Blake's depiction of mankind as the sleeping figure Albion, whose awakening is an apocalyptic event.

The point is worth pursuing, for in his preface Stapledon denies that his intent is to be literally prophetic or, at the other extreme, to write a purely fictional work which, though "aesthetically admirable," would not truly represent his vision of man's potential and limitations. Instead, he means to create a mythic image of man. Stapledon distinguishes between true and false myths:

A true myth is one which, within the universe of a certain culture (living or dead), expresses richly, and often perhaps tragically, the highest admirations possible within that culture. A false myth is one which either violently transgresses the limits of credibility set by its own cultural matrix, or expresses admirations less developed than those of its culture's best visions. This book can no more claim to be true myth than true prophecy. But it is an essay in myth creation. (9–10)

Robert Scholes has observed that Stapledon "sees future-fiction as a way of subjecting current values to a 'higher' set of values obtained by extrapolating from man's present 'admirations.' "[7] Believing that "our whole present mentality is but a confused and halting first experiment," Stapledon outlines the strengths and weaknesses of present-day man, as he sees them, and then develops a series of more or less detailed sketches of alternative forms of human culture. The large number of human species described in the book is necessary, for the point of the book is to force us to examine man's state objectively and dispassionately rather than assessing the human condition from our own limited point of view. Ultimately, we should try to see human history from a cosmic perspective so that we can rejoice even in the terrible beauty of man's inevitable end.

Yet *Last and First Men* is not merely a dispassionate appraisal of the human condition: at times it is also a sharply satiric work. The first of the artificial species, the Fourth Men or Great Brains, are grotesque monstrosities whose artificial skulls are concrete turrets forty feet in diameter. Described as a "preposterous factory of mind" and "a huge bump of curiosity equipped with most cunning hands," the first of the Great Brains is "wholly lacking in all normal instinctive responses, save curiosity and constructiveness" (203–4). The section devoted to the Great Brains is a relentlessly satiric attack on the inadequacies of a world view based entirely on scientific materialism, a school of thought which, according to Stapledon, leads inexorably to a reductive view of man and to the despair that results when we realize that there are no ultimate truths that can be based on a purely empirical view of the universe. Like Swift, who presented readers of *Gulliver's Travels* with a series of ironically conceived portraits of humanity, Stapledon exposes the folly of all simplistic images of man and the human condition. Neither pure bestiality nor pure rationalism—the Yahoos and Houyhnhnms of Swift's fable—is enough: Stapledon's ideal of humanity eludes all simple categories.

For this reason, perhaps, he makes the point that the Last Men are

"both more human and more animal" than we are: one of the First
Men would be likely to see the Last Men as "faun-like, and in
particular cases, ape-like, bear-like, ox-like, marsupial, or elephantine"
(274). The descriptions of this advanced race in bestial terms may be
contrasted with H. G. Wells's *The Island of Dr. Moreau,* in which a
crazed scientist speeds up the evolutionary process by surgically turning
animals into beast-men, each of whom retains characteristics of his
animal nature. When the horrified narrator, Prendick, returns to
London, he sees that we are all beast-people, that the beast lurks in
each of us beneath the thin veneer of civilization. Although Stapledon
found many reasons to praise Wells, he also took every opportunity to
criticize Wells's vision of man as being too narrowly based upon
biological considerations.[8] When we contrast the Great Brains, whose
animal nature has been almost entirely refined out of existence, with
the Last Men, in which the body contributes to man's total experience,
we see that reaction to Wells's materialistic conception of man is basic
to Stapledon's myth.

Stapledon traces the downfall of the Great Brains to a flaw in their
nature: their lack of emotions, and their inability to see man except in
the most materialistic terms. Other races, too, give way because of
crucial defects in their characters. A species of highly intelligent
monkeys who compete with the Second Men and almost annihilate
them are a case in point. They enslave the subhumans who are
descended from the group that left the Siberian colony to settle in
Labrador, but they are themselves slaves of their insane desire for
material wealth. Stapledon distinguishes them from the Second Men,
who "sought metal solely for the carrying on of an already well-
advanced civilization":

[T]he monkeys had no real use for metal. They merely hoarded it, and
became increasingly avaricious. No one had respect among them who did not
laboriously carry a great ingot about with him wherever he went. And after
a while it came to be considered actually indecent to be seen wihout a slab of
metal. In conversation between the sexes this symbol was always held so as to
conceal the genitals. (135)

Although the way the monkeys use the subhumans as cattle is
reminiscent of the relationship between the Houyhnhnms and Yahoos

in *Gulliver's Travels,* the monkeys' addiction to metal recalls one of the many weaknesses of the Yahoos rather than the calm rationality of the Houyhnhnms, and suggests that the monkeys are only a debased version of Swift's rational animals.[9] The monkeys' mania develops into a religious code as they increasingly use metal for such "sacred" purposes as covering genitalia; meanwhile, the idea of making weapons from metal is rejected on the grounds that to do so would be sacrilegious. Eventually the monkeys are overthrown by the subhumans whom they have enslaved, and the blame is laid upon their avarice: "The monkeys had so burdened their bodies with metal and their minds with the obsession of metal that at length the herds of subhuman cattle were able to rebel and devour their masters" (137).

A related yet superior obsession motivates the Martians who invade the Earth partly because they believe that diamonds are being misused on Earth. Existing in the form of vaporous clouds, the Martians worship the rigidity of diamonds and their ability to manipulate light rays. Clearly the Martian invasion represents an opportunity for both the Martians and the Second Men to broaden their horizons through contact with a different form of intelligent life; yet communication is blocked, first by the inability of each species to recognize that the other is intelligent, and later by a flaw in the Martians' mentality. The basic unit of Martian life is the individual cloudlet, yet in a crisis the whole race can become one great individual. Unfortunately, the Martian public mentality—the universal or racial mind—is inferior to the private mentality of the individual cloudlet, so when some of the Martian "colonists" begin to recognize that the terrestrials are intelligent beings and try to establish peaceful relations with them, the public mind on Mars, failing to make the imaginative leap needed to see the colonists' point of view, destroys the colony. Here, in addition to satirizing European colonial policies, Stapledon is dealing with one of his recurrent themes, the relation of the individual to the community: when it enforces a blind orthodoxy, the group mind actually retards the intellectual and spiritual development of each being. On the other hand, the racial mind of the Last Men allows each member of the race to retain his identity while rising to a new level of awareness. The question of community and the relation of the individual to the group are themes central to such later works as *Star Maker*.

The end of the Martian invasions comes only when the Second Men use germ warfare to destroy the Martians—and almost destroy themselves in the process. One of the most chillingly prophetic aspects of *Last and First Men* is the attention Stapledon pays to genocide, a term that did not even exist until fourteen years after the book was published, when Dr. Raphael Lemkin coined it to describe Hitler's attempt to murder an entire people. In Stapledon's myth, the Germans use poison gas against the Russians and later the Americans use poison gas against Europe; germ warfare is used, first, by the World State against rebellious workers, later by the super monkeys against the Second Men, and finally by the Second Men against the Martians; and the electrolysis that the Fifth Men use to create a breathable atmosphere on Venus results in the destruction of the native race of intelligent aquatic life. In general, Stapledon's attitude toward these episodes is consistent with his pacifistic leanings, but he treats the destruction of the Venerians more ambiguously: as it develops, the Venerians need radioactive material to exist, and since eventually there will be no more radioactive substances, "the Venerians were doomed, and man would merely hasten their destruction" (242). This defense failed to placate C. S. Lewis, who was so incensed by Stapledon's apparent endorsement of the extermination of the Venerians that he gave Weston, the villainous scientist of *Out of the Silent Planet,* a speech that lampoons Stapledon's ideas. The attack is not altogether fair, for Stapledon does not simply advocate killing even a doomed alien race in order to save humanity from certain destruction; what he shows, instead, is that scientific advances may present us with unforeseen moral problems, and that we cannot adequately face those problems without rising to a higher state of spiritual awareness. Of course there is no way out of the dilemma facing the Fifth Men, for if they do not continue the electrolysis they will all die and, inevitably, so will the Venerians. Even so, the decision helps to bring about a "racial neurosis" which contributes to the decline of the human race on Venus.

That decline is only one of many instances in which a human species degenerates toward a relatively barbaric state after reaching a high point in its culture. The high points—the stirrings of the sleeping figure Man before his final awakening—are, in the early stages, less extended than the dark ages between them. Stapledon is quite imaginative in the ways he discards the races he creates. The First Men destroy themselves, twice, through advanced technology that they are too spiritually immature to handle. The Second Men demolish their civilization through their war with the Martians. The Third Men are doomed by their artificially created successors, the Fourth Men, who in turn are deposed by their creation, the Fifth Men. In these early parts of the book, at least, it almost seems as if Stapledon agrees with Haldane that mankind can be the master of its fate and can save or doom itself, depending on the direction in which it develops its culture. But Stapledon later questions that position by introducing solar disasters beyond man's control that force man's evacuation to other planets and then bring an end to the solar system.

It may be worth noting that a similar dichotomy of thought exists in Wells's *The Time Machine*: at first it appears that the devolution of the human race into Eloi and Morlocks should be attributed directly to the inequalities of our social and economic systems, but later, when the Time Traveller watches the inexorable end of life on Earth as the whole solar system runs down, we realize that the physical law of entropy is at work in the degeneration of mankind, and that in a universe controlled by blind physical forces the destruction of the human race, though distant, is unavoidable. What distinguishes Stapledon from Wells, in this respect, is that Stapledon sees that man can triumph over, even though he cannot escape, the cold indifference of the physical universe. In fact, the work of perfecting the human spirit is especially urgent precisely because the end is so near: the narrator of *Last and First Men* tells us our future history in order to help bring about an evolution of the human spirit before the mad star puts an end to humanity.

That spiritual evolution can only come about when we see mankind from the broad perspective in which it is presented here, as well as through the narrower lens of our individual lives. From the broad view we learn that history is almost cyclic: patterns are repeated, but usually with a difference. The Sixth Men, for example, over a period of two hundred million years, recapitulate "all the main phases of man's life on earth," but "with characteristic differences" (248). Curtis C. Smith, commenting on the thematic importance of repetition in the novel, has observed that "a theme may be expressed perversely on one level but fully and marvelously on another. Flight is wasteful and self-destructive as performed by the religious fanatics of the First World State, but beautiful when the Seventh (flying) Men 'browse upon the bright pastures of the sky, like swallows.' "[10] The dispassionate ecstasy that the Seventh Men experience in the air is the means to a higher awareness, but it should be added that they are "awake" only when they are in flight: on the ground, the Seventh Men are pedestrian—figuratively as well as literally—and their inability to retain the insights they have experienced aloft often leads to despair. The division of their nature between their "awakened" selves when in flight and their "doltish" pedestrian lives anticipates Stapledon's development of this theme in later works, especially *A Man Divided,* his novel of a man whose split personality is representative of the human race on the verge of its ascent into a higher state of spiritual awareness.

The divided nature of the Seventh Men is also their central weakness—the reason for their ultimate downfall: their practical and spiritually awakened selves have no relation to one another, and when they are in the air they have no way of protecting themselves against the spiritually crippled but powerful and cunning pedestrian species that eventually overthrows them. Here, again, Stapledon adumbrates a later development of his theme, for in *Star Maker* the Plant Men have a divided nature, a spiritual or vegetable nature which is dominant while the sun is out and an animal nature that appears at night. The animal side is less spirtually developed than the plant side of their nature, but only the animal side can operate the machinery that keeps them safe in a world that is slowly losing its atmosphere. Eventually the failure to attend the life-support machinery during the day proves fatal.

Still another of Stapledon's repeated themes is human sexuality. In the early parts of the book, the emphasis falls upon the neurotic aspects of our sexual fears and desires, while toward the end, Stapledon stresses the liberating possibilities of sexual activity. Among the First

Men, sexuality all too often illustrates the possessiveness and insecurity that plague the race and lead, on a larger scale, to war: after the World State is destroyed, the quarrel in the Siberian colony that creates another division in the human species is, typically enough, the result of sexual jealousy. Stapledon's criticism of what he viewed as the sexual neurosis of English and American culture can be seen in the fact that the Anglo-French War of the late twentieth century is set off when an Englishwoman who has seduced a French African soldier claims that the Senegalese corporal actually raped her. Later, during the war, a brilliant peace initiative by the British government puts a temporary end to the killing, but hopes of permanent peace are shattered when a lone French pilot who does not realize that the war is over bombs the royal palace and kills a beautiful young princess: her body is grotesquely "impaled upon some high park-railings beside the main thoroughfare towards the city" (26). The symbolic rape of this "overwhelmingly potent sexual symbol and emblem of tribalism" so enrages the British that they return with a vengeance to their battle against the French.

Perhaps an even stronger, and more satiric, condemnation of the sexual conduct of the First Men occurs in the description of the World State, in which an annual "Sacred Lynching" becomes a popular ritual. The ceremony features a white woman and a black man whose dance ends with a ritual rape of the woman; when this is over, the Negro stabs the woman and attempts to escape to a sanctuary. If he makes it, he is viewed as a sacred person; if not, the mob kills him. This ceremony provides an outlet for the sexual impulses in a time when the knowledge and practice of sex are controlled to the extent of being reserved for those who have "won their wings" and are licensed to fly.

In contrast to these obvious perversions of the sexual instinct, other scenes treat sexuality more ambiguously. Before the founding of the World State, the planet is divided between Chinese and American factions that fight a war over Antarctic energy reserves. When the two sides hold a peace conference on a Pacific island, the envoys are interrupted by a beautiful multiracial woman who emerges nude from the ocean and calls herself the Daughter of Man. Propositioned by the Chinese representative and chastised for her nudity by the American, she nonetheless chooses to become the mistress of the American, whom she sees as the principle of energy. (This whole section of *Last and First Men* may be regarded as an allegory of man's divided nature, since the Chinese and the Americans represent the extremes of contemplative and active man, or thought and energy. The choice of the Daughter of Man, then, is symbolic of the wider choice of the human race and an omen of the Americanized planet of the First World State.)

Later the American becomes President of the World State, and his Vice-President, who wants to depose him, exposes his liaison with the multiracial beauty. But the President claims that it is his duty to have this affair, since it helps him to adopt the cosmopolitan viewpoint required by his office: "as President of the World, it was incumbent upon him to espouse the World. And since nothing could be said to be real without a physical basis, this spiritual union had to be embodied and symbolized by his physical union with the Daughter of Man" (71). Despite the obvious duplicity in the President's argument, Stapledon notes that "there was some truth in the plea that the Daughter of Man had enlarged the President's mind, for his policy had been unexpectedly tactful towards the East." That is to say, it is true that sexual activity is a potentially enlarging and liberating experience, although in the World State the conditions are not right for that experience to bear its proper fruit. What happens instead is that extramarital affairs gain a new superficial respectability: "Very soon it became fashionable to be a strict monogamist with one domestic wife, and one 'symbolical' wife in the East, or in another town, or a neighbouring street, or with several such in various localities" (72). A genuinely liberating revolution in attitudes toward human sexuality will have to wait for a later species, like the Last Men whose sexual groups allow each member of the group to enter into the experiences of all the other members and thereby to develop his own personality more fully.

The Last Men are Stapledon's most fully conceived example of "awakened" man, or man as the apotheosis of the human spirit. Individually they are impressive enough, with their giant stature, their incredibly long and varied lives, and their keen intellects, but they find their ultimate expression not in isolation but in the sexual groups and the racial experience. In these communal states the Last Men are able to probe the mysteries of the self, the race, and the cosmos, and their insight into these problems ranges so far beyond what we can comprehend that Stapledon's narrator is able to give us only a rough and abstract conception of it. A further hindrance is that, as the narrator puts it, "When we have declined from the racial mentality, we cannot clearly remember what it was that we experienced" (288–89). (Thus the Last Men all repeat, on a small scale, the ubiquitous pattern of rise and fall that afflicts mankind throughout the novel.) What the Last Men see, however, is that amidst the cold indifference of the universe there is meaning in the awakening and evolution of spirit, even though on the whole the moments when the human spirit is alive and awake are very brief. The problem is how to realize the "cosmic ideal," the perfect form of the cosmic spirit that will remain real in Eternity even though the material universe becomes chaotic: "For, if ever the cosmic ideal should be realized, even though for a moment only, then in that time the awakened Soul of All will embrace within itself all spirits whatever throughout the whole of time's wide circuit" (297). In this way, the Last Men hope to redeem the past and to lend meaning to the whole realm of human existence. Since their own civilization will be cut short by the "mad star," their hope is that another, more highly developed species somewhere in the universe will achieve the ideal which will elude them. Already, apparently, Stapledon had in mind the idea which he was later to develop into *Star Maker*.

Although the cosmic ideal is never realized in *Last and First Men*, it is clear that the pattern of development in the book reflects the evolution of the human spirit from its divided and chaotic beginnings among the First Men to the moment when, in their racial experience, the Last Men become one great man, and the sleeping figure outlined early in the book finally awakens. By beginning with a close examination of the immature First Men, whose divided spirit expresses itself in capitalistic exploitation and nationalistic wars, and concluding with the utopian world of the Last Men, Stapledon shows how far mankind has to go, yet he holds out the hope that the struggle will be successful and that we will someday awaken into the clearer state of perception that will provide answers for our many questions.

As an epic of the human spirit, *Last and First Men* is unparalleled in the field of science fiction: other contenders, such as the famous trilogies of C. S. Lewis, Isaac Asimov, and Frank Herbert, are pale by comparison. Stapledon's refusal to make concessions to popular taste guarantees that *Last and First Men* will never be a best-seller; but even so, the beauty of its language, the startling range of imagination that it displays, and the importance of its theme assure that *Last and First Men* will have a devoted readership long after more popular but less imaginatively conceived novels have lost the power to enchant their readers.

Far Future Calling (1930/1978)

Shortly after completing his first novel, Stapledon distilled the essence of *Last and First Men* into a radio play entitled *Far Future Calling*. The script of this brief play reveals that Stapledon had considerable skill in handling the medium of radio. The play actually begins as a radio play: an actor and an actress are reading the script of an inane comedy about life in A.D. 2500. But their dialogue is interrupted by one of the Last Men, who puts an end to the play and uses his mental powers to silence the actor and actress until they agree to cooperate with him. The future man, who is soon joined by a future woman, gives the radio performers a view of the world of the Last Men; the radio audience experiences that world secondhand, through the reactions of the actor and the actress. Hence there are really two levels of broadcasting going on: the Last Men are beaming their message to the performers, and the B.B.C. is sending the program out to radios across Britain. Moreover, there are occasional interruptions in which the actor and actress see and hear events that take place during other stages of man's long history. The future woman explains that "It's something like listening in to radio messages. Our selectivity is not quite good enough to prevent interference."[11] As a result, we catch glimpses of the flying Seventh Men, of the Great Brains, and of a scene that may be from the Euro-American War of the First Men. The play culminates in an apocalyptic vision of the racial experience of the Last Men, after which the transmission fades and the performers find themselves alone again in the radio studio.

It may seem curious that Stapledon wrote a radio play at all, since his fundamental distrust of radio is evident in several of his works. On the one hand, radio is an altogether too convenient medium for propaganda broadcasts in favor of despotic governments or powerful private interests, while on the other hand it may be reduced to carrying little more than the most insipid sort of popular entertainment. The latter possibility is satirized in the "cheap fantasy of five hundred years hence" that the B.B.C. is broadcasting at the beginning of *Far Future Calling*; in addition, this sequence reveals Stapledon's capacity for parody, since it is actually an ironic version of the more serious theme that the Last Men want to transmit. Despite the possibility that the medium could be corrupted or trivialized, however, *Far Future Calling* demonstrates its author's conviction that radio could be used creatively and intelligently. While the play was never put on the air, and was not published until 1978, the experience of writing it was useful not merely because it gave Stapledon some insight into the problems of adapting his theme to another medium and a different sort of audience, but also because he was able to rescue several passages and incorporate them into his next novel, *Last Men in London*.

Last Men in London (1932)

Although in his preface to *Last Men in London* Stapledon contends that "This book is intelligible without reference to another fantasy . . . called *Last and First Men*" (9),[12] readers will discover that the sequel is primarily of interest as an extension and clarification of ideas developed in the earlier novel. Indeed, judged strictly on its own merits apart from the other works, *Last Men in London* is one of the least successful of Stapledon's science fiction novels. Even so, the book deserves more attention than it has received, for several reasons: because it provides us with some of the clearest statements of Stapledon's assessment of the human condition in the twentieth century; because the character of Paul is partly the author's self-portrait; and because parts of the novel anticipate themes developed in such later books as *Odd John* and *A Man Divided*.

The narrator of *Last Men in London* is the same Last Man who spoke across the span of two billion years in *Last and First Men*. In general he is concerned with three subjects: the world of the Last Men, the analysis of the history of the First Men up to World War I, and the personal history of a particular twentieth-century man known as Paul. Throughout most of the book the narrator speaks to us from a point in time after the narration of the main part of *Last and First Men* but before the epilogue of that book; at the end of *Last Men in London*, however, there is another epilogue, narrated directly by "the terrestrial author of this book," which includes a message that Stapledon claims to have pieced together from an attempted transmission thousands of years after the epilogue of the first book. At this point the "mad star" has wreaked such havoc upon the Last Men that the entire culture is disintegrating. The beauty of the passage is its attempt to capture the pathos of this disintegration. The narrator has declined so far from his earlier enlightened state that in his misery he mocks the ending of *Last and First Men:* before, he says, "we faced all things gaily. Even this corruption, when we foresaw it, we called 'a fair end to the brief music that is man'. This! The strings all awry, screaming out of tune, a fair end!" (268).

The opening section of the book is notable for its close examination of the Last Men (including an autobiographical sketch by the Neptunian narrator) and for its description of the method of mental time traveling used by the narrator and other explorers of the past. The Portal to the Past, where all the exploration takes place, is located underground in a remote arctic region on Neptune where telepathic vibrations from minds of other Last Men will not interfere with the vulnerable mind of the time-explorer. In his journey to the past, the explorer first assumes the mentality of a particular culture and then selects a mind of an individual being within the time period that he is drawn to. (A similar idea operates in *Star Maker* when the cosmic traveler is attracted first to the Other Earth and later to other nonhuman cultures.) This time, the narrator finds himself in London at the beginning of World War I, in the mind of Paul, the character who will be the vehicle for Stapledon's examination of modern man.

Paul is chosen for study not because he is an average man—he really is not average, as the narrator says—but because "he is typical in that he illustrates very clearly the confused nature of his species, and the disorder of its world" (63). Paul is one of Stapledon's many examples of man torn between the forces of darkness and light, or as the narrator phrases it, "between the primitive simian nature and the

genuinely human." Paul's unseen Neptunian visitor strengthens the
"genuinely human" part of his nature by giving him occasional
insights into his own world, and even giving him glimpses of the world
of the Last Men, from the superior Neptunian point of view. The
result of this influence is the creation of two almost separate
personalities, somewhat like the "doltish" and "awakened" personalities which both occupy the body of Victor Smith in *A Man Divided*.
After considerable confusion and doubt about his own motives as well
as the war itself, Paul enlists in an ambulance corps; one of his
companions is none other than Olaf Stapledon, whom the narrator
describes rather ironically as "the colourless but useful creature whom
I have chosen as my mouthpiece for communicating with you" (175).
After the war the narrator arranges for Paul to have an affair that
relieves him of sexual anxiety and frustration. As part of his continuing
effort to awaken Paul into a higher state of awareness and sympathy,
the narrator finally reveals his presence in the mind of his host.
Although understandably uneasy about having another being observe
his every thought, Paul eventually accepts the narrator's presence and
is able to approximate the detached cosmical point of view of the Last
Men.

If *Last Men in London* were as coherent as this précis indicates, it
would be a more successful novel. Unfortunately the book lacks the
clear outline of *Last and First Men*: Stapledon even interrupts his
analysis of Paul's life to spend about fifty pages describing the forces
in human history that led to World War I. Although this section is of
some interest as part of what Cyril M. Kornbluth has called
Stapledon's "detailed indictment of contemporary life" in this novel,[13]
it is for the most part an example of the sort of writing that works
better in Stapledon's nonfictional books. Still, if the whole is severely
flawed, parts are brilliant. One of these parts is the description of a
prehistoric race of "philosophical lemurs" whose spiritual development
outstrips anything in our civilization. The lemurs are actually a mirror
image of modern man: the practical and material aspects of their
culture lag far behind their spiritual insight, while in the twentieth
century, man is too spiritually immature to cope with the advanced
technological environment that he has created. Eventually the lemurs
are destroyed by "a hardier and a more extravert species," man's

"half-simian ancestors" whose ruthless aggressiveness allows them to survive while the more spiritually advanced lemurs become extinct (128). The struggle between the lemurs and the ape-men symbolizes the ongoing struggle in the twentieth century between the "human" and "simian" halves of man's nature—his desire for enlightenment and community, on the one hand, and his relapse into the cult of selfhood on the other. The war, the worship of heroes, the general disregard of all but the most conventional ideas, and the ancient example of the defeat of the lemurs all indicate that once again man's chance to achieve spiritual greatness will be doomed.

Perhaps the most brilliantly developed aspect of *Last Men in London* is the recurrent image of the half-born foal. The image is first inserted in Paul's mind by the narrator:

Another image haunted [Paul] in connexion with these faces [of his contemporaries], and seemed to him to summarize them all and symbolize the condition of his species. . . . He seemed to see, lying in mud, a dead mare, already decaying. From its hindquarters, which were turned towards him, there projected the hideously comical face of its unborn foal. The first time he encountered this apparition Paul was at a political meeting. . . . Suddenly Paul saw the foal, and in a flash recognized its expression in the speaker, in the ladies and gentlemen on the platform, in the audience. His gorge rose, he thought he was going to vomit. (108)

The foal image recalls the famous lines from Matthew Arnold's "Stanzas from the Grande Chartreuse," where Arnold imagined himself "Wandering between two worlds, one dead, / The other powerless to be born." Just as Arnold symbolized the spiritual crisis of the Victorian era in his poem, Stapledon attempts to represent the spiritual crisis of modern man in his frequent references to the foal.

Like all literary images, the foal and its mare work on several levels at once. On its most general level, the foal represents whatever is truly human and spiritual in man, while the dead mare represents all of man's lower ("simian") instincts—including the militaristic heroism that thrives on war—which will not allow the birth of man's higher self. Paul sees other meanings as well: "Sometimes it seemed to him that he himself was the foal, unable to free himself from the restriction of an outgrown mentality. Sometimes the whole human race was the foal. Sometimes on the other hand, the foal was just his unborn martial self throttled by his most unmartial past" (171). The last of these interpretations is the least likely, for the martial ideal is more accurately seen in the dead mare strangling the modern world. That becomes clear when, during the war, he finally comes upon the scene that has appeared in his imagination for years:

Paul one day perceived in a field by the road the mare and unborn foal whose image had so long haunted him. The unexpected but all too familiar sight shocked him deeply. Volume by volume it corresponded with his image, but there was an added stench. . . .

One symbolical aspect of his foal was still hidden from him. When at last the armistice came, so longed for, so incredible, Paul did not yet know that the peace ensuing on the world's four years' travail was to be the peace, not of accomplished birth but of strangulation. (188)

Hence in the end the mare becomes the war and the mentality it symbolizes, while the foal represents the postwar years in which the hope that the world war would indeed end war was drowned by the nationalism that ultimately led to another world war.[14] Seeing the foal first in his imagination and then in the external world, Paul comes to understand that he is a microcosm of humanity and that his crisis is somehow that of mankind in general. Yet through the influence of his Neptunian visitor, Paul ultimately is able to rise above the crisis and to view his situation, and the world's, more objectively. Thus while the war "undermine[s] man's confidence in his own nature" and produces "a kind of racial neurosis blended of guilt, horror, inferiority, and hate" (154), Paul learns to find new meaning both in his own life and in the life of the species.

Before the war, Paul, following Stapledon's example, becomes a teacher. He proves incompetent, but when he returns to teaching after the war he improves rapidly. Later he becomes headmaster of a school where one of his students, an apparently stupid and lazy boy named Humpty, turns out to be so extraordinarily intelligent and perceptive that he may almost be regarded as belonging to another, superhuman, species. Humpty is one of many examples of superior beings produced by genetic mutation; like the others, he is profoundly alienated by the basic stupidity of "normal" human society and by the way he has been mistreated because of his inability to be like everyone else. The simian metaphor that Stapledon uses throughout *Last Men in London* reappears in this section to underline the difference between the supernormals and the rest of human society: the narrator notes that the supernormals develop slowly in comparison to other people, just as people develop more slowly than apes (247). Moreover, "Each of them was like an isolated human child brought up by apes in the jungle. When at last he had begun to realize the gulf between himself and others, he realized also that he had been damaged past repair by his simian upbringing" (253). Finally, Humpty's role in the school is compared to that of "a naturalist in the jungle studying the mentality of apes" (256). This metaphor suggests the influence of Nietzsche, whose Superman is as much an advance over man as man is over his simian ancestors.[15] Humpty is a Nietzschean character in other ways, too, for his revolt is directed against the conventional mind and its moral code. Yet he is unable to carry out his plan of action— reforming the world, perhaps by founding a colony of supernormals that "would become the germ of a new human species and a new world-order" (258)—because he is a twisted being, motivated not merely by a sense of the rightness of his cause but by a hatred of the society in which he is doomed to be a stranger. Out of despair, he kills himself.

Humpty's death is tragic, yet his life is a hopeful sign. Stapledon implies as much in his final reference to this episode:

> Thus ended one of Nature's blundering attempts to improve upon her first, experimental, humanity. One other superior and much more fortunate individual was destined almost to succeed in the task that Humpty had merely imagined. Of this other, of the utopian colony which he founded, and its destruction by a jealous world, I may tell on another occasion. (261)

When the occasion for telling that story came a few years later, the result was Olaf Stapledon's next major novel, and one of his best: *Odd John*.

Chapter Three
More Than Human
The Superman Theme

Two major recurrent themes of science fiction are the concept of the superman and the vision of a utopian world. It is not hard to see why these themes are so often found in tandem: as the superman is the apotheosis of individual man, the utopian society is the most highly advanced form of communal man. Given the broad view of *Last and First Men,* it is particularly appropriate that in that book the superior man most often emerges as a race—e.g., the Fifth Men or the Last Men—and creates an advanced society which in turn helps to reinforce all of the "awakened" features of its members. Nonetheless, the character known as Humpty in *Last Men in London,* and prophets like the Divine Boy of Patagonia in *Last and First Men,* are evidence that the superman and utopia are not inseparable. What these characters also show is that when *Homo superior* is born into the world of *Homo sapiens,* he can find himself alienated from the rest of mankind; in an extreme case like Humpty's, the alienation can produce madness or despair.

The theme of the superior (and often alienated) individual, which is evident in many of Stapledon's works, became the focus of two of his finest novels: *Odd John* (1935), the story of a superman whose great intelligence is the result of a natural mutation, and *Sirius* (1944), which chronicles the life of a dog with superhuman mentality. For many of the ideas developed in these books, Stapledon drew upon two main sources: the Nietzschean concept of the *Übermensch* or superman, and the tradition of the superman in science fiction. Although these concepts are related, it will be most convenient to deal with them separately.

The influence of Friedrich Nietzsche on *Odd John* is both evident and complex. As a socialist, Stapledon would have had little sympathy for Nietzsche's aristocratic leanings, or for his contemptuous attitude toward the masses whom Nietzsche termed "the much-too-many"; it is particularly difficult to imagine Stapledon praising Cesare Borgia, as Nietzsche did. Moreover, Stapledon believed that the spiritual development of man was inseparable from a general improvement in the conditions of life for all people, while Nietzsche argued that "the abolition of these evils [vice, illness, prostitution, poverty] was neither possible nor even desirable, since they have belonged and will belong to all periods of human history."[1] Yet like Nietzsche, Stapledon found himself in revolt against nihilism, against the conformist mentality of the bourgeois world, and against purely scientific and reductive views of mankind. It is also likely that Stapledon's concept of the relation of man and superman was shaped partly by passages like the following from *Thus Spoke Zarathustra:*

Man is a rope, fastened between animal and Superman—a rope over an abyss.

A dangerous going-across, a dangerous wayfaring, a dangerous looking-back, a dangerous shuddering and staying-still.

What is great in man is that he is a bridge and not a goal; what can be loved in man is that he is a *going-across* and a *down-going.*[2]

Perhaps the two ideas which most closely relate Nietzsche and Stapledon are that the superman is certain to be misunderstood and distrusted by the great mass of humanity, and that the superman is not necessarily bound by the same code of morality that applies to other men. The moral dimensions of Stapledon's concept of the superman involve such complexities that a full discussion must be postponed until later in this chapter. On the other hand, the alienation of the superman from the rest of mankind is a theme found in science fiction novels ever since the publication of Mary Shelley's *Frankenstein* (1818). One of the ironies of *Frankenstein* is that the monster is in many ways superior to the people whose company and love he so desperately wants—Frankenstein and the others who fear and despise him: not only is he larger, faster, more powerful, and more intelligent than other people, but along with our awareness of his tragic loneliness comes a feeling that, as Harold Bloom puts it, "the monster is *more human* than his creator."[3]

The separation of the superman from mankind as a whole takes many different forms in other novels. In H. G. Wells's *The Food of the Gods* (1904),[4] the giants raised on "Boomfood" are drawn into mortal combat with the Lilliputian forces of mankind; likewise, in A. E. van Vogt's *Slan* (1940) the government's official objective is the extinction of the superior slan race. In Robert A. Heinlein's *Methuselah's Children* (1941; revised and expanded 1958) the long-lived human beings who make up the Families are forced into exile because of an erroneous popular belief that they possess the secret of longevity, while in Zenna Henderson's *Pilgrimage* (1961) the People, extraterrestrial beings living on Earth, have suffered persecution as witches because of their ability to fly. Again and again, the message of the science fiction novel is that man always resents and distrusts the superman. The point is perhaps demonstrated most dramatically in Heinlein's *Stranger in a Strange Land* (1961), where Valentine Michael Smith—"a combination of Captain Marvel and Christ," as Scholes and Rabkin call him[5]—is murdered by a mob because the religion that he founds presents a fundamental challenge to conventional religion and morality, and because, ultimately, the superiority of the superman proves intolerable. In Philip Wylie's *Gladiator* (1930), Hugo Danner saves Roseanne Cane from a charging bull by breaking the bull's neck, but instead of being grateful she is frightened by Danner's strength: as she says, "It isn't natural to be able to do things like that. It isn't human."[6] From that terrible fear of whatever "isn't human," the superman has no escape.

Although many books must have influenced *Odd John,* its true progenitor—one that Stapledon acknowledges in the pages of his book—is J. D. Beresford's classic novel, *The Hampdenshire Wonder* (1911).[7] Beresford's novel and Stapledon's are alike in a number of superficial ways: both books are supposed to be biographies written by journalists who have fallen under the spell of their subjects; Victor Stott—the Wonder—and John Wainwright both educate themselves at least partly by memorizing dictionaries and other reference books; both boys have large heads and unusual eyes, and both are at one point assumed to be retarded because they do not develop in the way "normal" children do. But the real similarity between the Wonder and Odd John lies in the shape of their mentality, for both boys are so intellectually advanced that they must be regarded as belonging to another—to a superhuman—species. This mental difference then forms the basis for the more awakened spirits of the superhuman characters and for their profound sense of alienation from the human race.

Stapledon sets out one of the major differences between his novel and Beresford's when he writes: "How pathetically one-sided the supernormal development may be is revealed in Mr. J. D. Beresford's account of the unhappy Victor Stott. I hope that the following brief record will at least suggest a mind at once more strikingly 'superhuman' and more broadly human" (6).[8] Partly because *Odd John* is an attempt to get at ideas beyond the comprehension of most if not all readers, and partly because (like many of Stapledon's books) it depends heavily on summation and dialogue and has few dramatically intense scenes, the novel is somewhat flawed. (These defects, however, are reduced, and to a large extent eliminated, in *Sirius*.) Yet as Isaac Asimov has noted, *Odd John* is an exceptional novel because in it the superman "is so skilfully drawn that he really seems both nonhuman and superhuman."[9] Moreover, Stapledon realized, perhaps more than any other writer, that a superhuman character would not simply think faster or better than other people, but that his mind would be fundamentally different from ours: while the supernormal protagonist of Wilmar Shiras's *Children of the Atom* (1953) believes in the Boy Scout Law and attends church regularly, John Wainwright develops his own vision of the human condition, learning little of any importance from previous religions or philosophies. The value of *Odd John*, then, lies both in the thorough and convincing portrait of John's superior mind and his growing alienation from mankind, and in the use of this character and his situation to develop a wide-ranging criticism of many aspects of our civilization. Later, when the feat is repeated in *Sirius*, it is even more successful.

Odd John: The Crisis

Narrated by a free-lance journalist who describes himself as "a respectable member of the English middle class," *Odd John* is the history of a superhuman being whose very existence constitutes a challenge to "normality." John Wainwright, the "odd" member of an otherwise unremarkable English family, develops erratically, conceiving a theory of relativity at the age of five but not learning to walk until the age of six. As he grows, he becomes increasingly aware that he is unlike most other people, but eventually he begins to establish contact with other supernormals from distant parts of the world. Gathered together upon a Pacific island, twenty-two supernormal children found a secret utopian colony, but after a few years they are discovered and harassed by governments of the world they have fled. Rather than abandon their colony and return to the "normal" world, the colonists commit mass suicide by exploding the island so that it sinks beneath the waves.[10]

Odd John has been described as "a powerfully evocative communication of the spirit in crisis,"[11] and the deaths of the colonists certainly suggest one aspect of the spiritual crisis of our age: the triumph of the doltish conformity or subhuman mentality of the millions over the superhuman intelligence of the awakened few. Yet unlike Humpty, whose brilliant but twisted mind leads to despair, John Wainwright and his fellow colonists are motivated by an ecstatic acceptance of their fate, a conviction that they have played a significant role in the life of the spirit. Whereas Humpty lives an apparently pointless life of unrewarded suffering, John finds beauty, love, and meaning in the twenty-three years of his brief but intense existence. Still, as an alien in the world of *Homo sapiens,* John suffers through a series of crises that symbolize the conflict of the subhuman and the superhuman (or, as Stapledon would have it, the "truly human") forces, both within him and within mankind generally.

Two incidents—the murder of a policeman and the slaying of a stag—will illustrate the nature of the spiritual crisis that John faces and the pattern of his spiritual development. Both events derive ultimately from John's estrangement from the rest of mankind and his search for his own identity apart from the norms of human society. The first occurrence, the murder of a constable, is the unforeseen outcome of John's brief career as a second-story man. Initially, at least, John has no doubts about the morality of burglary: he sees it as a way to gain money and experience at the same time, and he argues that "Mr. Magnate [a rich capitalist] and his like [are] fair game" (31). Yet his decision to rob the rich brings him to a more difficult, and unexpected, moral decision when he is caught by Smithson, a friendly police constable whom John knows. Faced with the choice of killing himself, going to jail, or murdering Smithson, John chooses the last alternative in the belief that the other choices would betray his task of advancing the spirit on Earth. He is motivated not simply by faith in his mission but by a sudden realization that there is a spiritual dimension to his superiority over the rest of humanity:

I had already, some time before, come to think of myself as definitely of a different biological species from *Homo sapiens,* the species of that amiable bloodhound behind the torch [Smithson]. But at last I realized for the first time that this difference carried with it what I should now describe as a far-reaching spiritual difference, that my purpose in life, and my attitude to life, were to be different from anything which the normal species could conceive, that I stood, as it were, on the threshold of a world far beyond the reach of those sixteen hundred million crude animals that at present ruled the planet. (32)

The justification for the murder, then, rests largely on John's belief in his superiority over other men and in the superiority of his mission. (The description of men in animal terms in the quotation above is echoed when John compares his regret over Smithson's death to the feeling he had once before when he killed a mouse [33]; the suggestion is that from John's perspective, man is not much greater than the mouse.) In a superficial way this incident recalls Dostoevsky's *Crime and Punishment,* but the parallels only serve to highlight the crucial differences between Dostoevsky's self-styled superman and Stapledon's Odd John. For one thing, Raskolnikov kills the old pawnbroker woman largely to prove to himself that he is superior to others and that the ordinary moral laws do not apply to him any more than (in his mind) they apply to Napoleon. He steals money from her, but this seems an afterthought: he does not absolutely need her money, and in any case he is so afraid of being caught that he buries the money and never uses any of it. In short, Raskolnikov commits a senseless murder. By comparison, John's murder of Smithson is clearly motivated. A more important difference, though, is that Raskolnikov is really *not* superior to others—he learns, in fact, that he is in some ways inferior to other people and that he must suffer in order to redeem himself—while John is demonstrably superhuman.

At the time of the murder, John sees that he "must set about the more practical side of [his] task either by taking charge of the common species and teaching it to bring out the best in itself, or, if that proved impossible, by founding a finer type of [his] own" (32). Later, after carrying out a thorough examination of humanity, he declares "*Homo sapiens* is at the end of his tether, and I'm not going to spend my life tinkering a doomed species" (70). Retreating to a mountainous area, John learns to live entirely apart from human civilization and to rely entirely on his own devices. The climax of his retreat is the slaying of a magnificent stag, a symbolic action that Roger Brunet interprets as John's triumph over "the subhuman in man that refuses to be killed in generation after generation, causing war after war." Brunet notes that

John is able to kill [the stag], to come at once to terms with nature and through nature to man and his own identity, because he is John, potentially 'fully human,' free of the repetitive cycle of self-destruction that is the fate of normal men. When John kills the stag he dominates nature (obtains food) and dominates on a symbolic level the *homo sapiens* species, the normal human. It is in fact the superhuman dominating the normal and the subhuman within himself: it is the achievement of self-mastery.[12]

The death of the stag, then, represents a spiritual triumph, an awakening, just as the half-born and half-dead foal in *Last Men in London* represents the defeat of man's spirit and the triumph of the subhuman over the fully human in man. John's triumph leads to a new awakening, for he suddenly sees mankind from a new perspective. His disgust with *Homo sapiens* is replaced with a sudden understanding of man's spiritual plight: sensitive to pain but unable to achieve the detached viewpoint of the superman, man is doomed to suffer without being able to understand why. Having seen men merely as beasts, John comes to realize that man "was indeed a spirit of a higher order than any beast, though in the main obtuse, heartless, unfaithful to the best in himself" (83). Thus when his hideout is discovered by two mountain climbers, he recalls the beautiful but doomed stag: "suddenly the stag seemed to symbolize the whole normal human species, as a thing with a great beauty and dignity of its own, and a rightness of its own, so long as it was not put into situations too difficult for it" (84). Unfortunately, "the present world-situation" has proved to be beyond man's capacities: "The thought of *Homo sapiens* trying to run a mechanized civilization suddenly seemed to him as ludicrous and pathetic as the thought of a stag in the driving-seat of a motor-car."

Throughout this section, Stapledon's theme is reminiscent of his criticism of the First Men in *Last and First Men* and *Last Men in London.* In those books, Stapledon contends that man's animal nature is fundamentally in conflict with the demands of the world-community and of modern technology: again and again nationalism, militarism, chauvinism, and other subhuman elements prevent man's awakening into a higher awareness. Narrated by a superior being, one of the Last Men, both of the earlier novels are supposed to be aimed at First Men who cannot comprehend fully the meaning of the books but can be given glimpses of the future in order that they may become more alert to beauty and truth. The process is especially clear in *Last Men in London,* where the narrator gives Paul occasional glimpses of the future that subtly change his character as he adopts a more "Neptunian" point of view; *Far Future Calling,* of course, is devoted to the same principle. Likewise, in *Odd John,* after he is discovered in the cave, John performs a "miracle": he lifts a gigantic boulder and allows the two mountain climbers a clear look at the starry sky (76). Later, called on to explain, John says that

"The important thing was that, when I did see the stars (riotously darting in all directions according to the caprice of their own wild natures, yet in every movement confirming the law), the whole tangled horror that had tormented me finally presented itself to me in its true and beautiful shape. And I knew that the first, blind stage of my childhood had ended." (85)

The vision of the stars symbolizes John's awakening from the dark night of the soul into the self-detached ecstasy of the cosmic or "Neptunian" point of view. In sharing this vision with normal men, John affirms his own humanity and his sense of his mission in life. Reacting against the temptation to nihilism, John realizes that he must dedicate himself to the awakening of spirit throughout the world. From this point on he concentrates on searching for and bringing together others of his kind, and on creating the colony that will permit each of its members to develop fully without the restraining and perverting influence of the "normal" or subhuman world.

The Colony

John's search for other supernormals gives Stapledon an opportunity to describe a wide variety of responses to the normal world. At one extreme are John's first two discoveries: James Jones, a lunatic whose only coherent form of expression is a music so subtle that it can only be appreciated by one like himself, and a Hebridean cripple who has become so twisted, frustrated, and filled with hatred that he tries to destroy John's mind. Like Humpty, these beings find life among *Homo sapiens* a source of torment, just as we might be driven into insanity if we were forced to live in a world controlled by apes or idiots. At the other extreme are the particularly well-balanced beings who, through good fortune, have escaped psychological scarring: Jacqueline, a French prostitute who "combined in her person the functions of harlot, psycho-analyst and priest" (105) and who at the age of 165 still appears a young woman; Adlan, an Egyptian who died thirty-five years earlier but still manages to make mental contact with John; Langatse, a blind Tibetan monk who is able to see telepathically by using the eyes of other people; and dozens more. Among the others are the twenty-two with whom John founds his colony.

Like the advanced societies of *Last and First Men,* the Pacific colony of *Odd John* is an idealized world with all the best features of communism and individualism. John criticizes the standard brand of communism as too "rationalistic, scientific, mechanistic, brass-tack-istic" (63), that is, for failing to see the spiritual impulse behind dialectical materialism, just as he might have censured Nietzsche for not recognizing the need for an economic basis for man's spiritual development. When a Russian ship arrives to offer the colonists sanctuary in the Soviet Union, John spells out the differences between the form of communism practiced on the island and the communism of the Bolshevik state:

"Yes," said John, laughing, "Comrades, you have the wrong approach. Like you, we are Communists, but we are other things also. For you, Communism is the goal, but for us it is the beginning. For you the group is sacred, but for us it is only the pattern made up of individuals. Though we are Communists, we have reached beyond Communism to a new individualism. Our Communism is individualistic. In many ways we admire the achievements of the New Russia; but if we were to accept this offer we should very soon come into conflict with your Government. From our point of view it is better for our colony to be destroyed than to be enslaved by any alien Power." (151)

On the broad level, then, the colony is a reaction against the conformism both of the capitalist state and of the communist state: John and the others are always aware that the group "is only the pattern made up of individuals" and that their differences from one another are at least as important as their similarities. The aim is to engender and nourish "personality-in-community," an idea based on our recognition of the essential "otherness" of our fellows: as Stapledon says elsewhere, "In the truly human kind of social behaviour there is clear awareness of the other as a person, different from oneself in character, temperament, needs, capacities; and these differences are accepted, nay welcomed." Hence the relationship of the awakened or superior individual and the utopian society can be seen clearly, for "true community is impossible save as the community of mutually aware and mutually respecting persons. But on the other hand, personality itself cannot exist, in any form worthy of the name, save as 'persons-in-community.' "[13] If the refusal or inability of "normal" society to recognize and accept the otherness of the supernormals is largely to blame for the twisted mind of the Hebridean cripple and for James Jones's lunacy, precisely the reverse is true in the colony, where the recognition and acceptance of differences helps to create a symbiotic relationship among the colonists.

"The true purpose of the awakened spirit," the colonists tell the narrator, "is twofold, namely to help in the practical task of world-building, and to employ itself to the best of its capacity in intelligent worship" (144). The colony itself is an attempt to fuse the active and the contemplative aspects of the life of the awakened spirit. The active side of their life consists of all the outward life of the island: eugenic experimentation, research into the relationship of mind and matter, the production of art objects, and especially the reformation of the economic and social life of the island along the lines of utopian communism. But when the colony is discovered and is brought to the attention of the six "Pacific Powers"—Britain, France, the United States, Holland, Japan, and Russia—the islanders realize that they will not be allowed to proceed with their work toward the remaking of man and his world. With a clear-minded and ecstatic acceptance of fate (reminiscent of the attitude of the Last Men before their minds are destroyed by the mad star's radiation), they turn to the life of contemplation and praise, hoping to "offer to the universal Spirit such a bright and peculiar jewel of worship as even the great Langatse himself, alone and thwarted, could not create" (144–45).

Whether or not the colonists create that "jewel of worship" is not clear, for here (as in the conclusions of *Last and First Men* and *Star Maker*) Stapledon is reaching for ideas so far beyond the range of realistic fiction that they can be described only in the most abstract terms. Constant interruptions from the outside world—first by the navies of the Pacific Powers, later by hired assassins—disrupt their concentration, forcing them away from the life of contemplation and praise, but when they commit suicide by destroying their island, the narrator, following events from afar, hopes that they have achieved their aim:

I suspected that the islanders had been holding their assailants at bay in order to gain a few days for the completion of their high spiritual task, or in order to bring it at least to a point beyond which there was no hope of further advancement. I liked to believe that during the few days after the repulse of the third landing-party they accomplished this aim. They then decided, I thought, not to await the destruction which was bound sooner or later to overtake them at the hands of the less human species. . . . They would not allow their home, and all the objects of beauty with which they had adorned it, to fall into subhuman clutches. Therefore they deliberately blew up their power-station. . . . (156–57)

Whatever the ultimate value of John Wainwright's life, it is clear that in the communal life of the colony, and particularly in his relationship with Lo, a supernormal girl whose love for him seems to be consummated only at the very end, he has discovered a meaning and purpose in life and in death. Yet John achieves his final attitude of ecsasy in the face of oblivion only through the awakened community of supernormal peers. By contrast, near the end of *Sirius* the great dog realizes that "There is no place for me in man's world, and there is no other world for me. There is no place for me anywhere in the universe" (306). Because he has no community of peers, because his divided nature is at home neither in the world of man nor in the world of the wolf, Sirius endures frustration and torment greater than John ever knows. And his story, which Aldiss half-ironically calls "the most human of all Stapledon's novels,"[14] reexamines from another (and a more original) angle all of the questions raised in *Odd John*.

Sirius: A Dog Divided

In "Tobermory," one of the finest satiric fantasies of H. H. Munro ("Saki"), Cornelius Appin teaches a tomcat to speak. Appin considers his discovery more important than the invention of the printing press, but the experiment backfires when it develops that Tobermory knows, and loves to repeat, all of the things that nobody wants told: whose bedroom Major Barfield has frequented, what Lady Blemley said about Mavis Pellington, and the like.[15] Saki's story is a recent example of a traditional plot motif that is perhaps best illustrated by *The Golden Ass* of Apuleius, in which Lucius is transformed into an ass and forced to remain in that condition for a year until he is released through the agency of Isis and Osiris. Like Tobermory, Lucius has ample opportunity to observe the worst in human behavior since people normally assume that an animal cannot understand, much less report, what they are doing and saying.

To a certain extent, the same possibilities are exploited in *Sirius*, Stapledon's novel about a sheep dog whose intelligence is at least human (and in some ways superhuman). The narrator observes that "One cause of Sirius's incipient contempt for human beings was the fact that since they thought he was 'only an animal,' they often gave themselves away badly in his presence" (225–26). Almost in the manner of an invisible man, Sirius watches the hypocrisy and cruelty of mankind and, from his alien point of view, develops a sophisticated understanding of the spiritual condition of modern man. Yet *Sirius* is not simply a satiric portrait of humanity. Rather, the novel is "a fantasy of love and discord," as Stapledon subtitled it, and its true value lies in the portrayal of the deep spiritual conflicts produced in the mind of this great dog who, like Frankenstein's monster, has no mate, no companion of his own kind.

The comparison with *Frankenstein* is suggested in part by a biblical analogy. In Mary Shelley's novel the creature finds and reads a copy of *Paradise Lost* and comes to see that "Like Adam, I was apparently united by no link to any other being in existence."[16] Sirius regards himself in similar terms when he asks his creator, "Why did you make *me* without making a world for me to live in. It's as though God had made Adam and not bothered to make Eden, nor Eve" (222). In both books, too, the analogy has a darker side: Frankenstein's monster comes to see himself as Satan warring against the human world that has rejected him, while Sirius, who is thought by superstitious people to be a devil in the shape of a dog, periodically rebels against the same world of men. Yet the form of the monster's Satanic revolt—"Evil thenceforth became my good"[17]—is at heart a simplistic reversal of values deriving from his exclusion from human society. Unlike Frankenstein's monster, Sirius is neither rejected by his creator nor deprived of human love and affection, but he is always a stranger in a strange land, completely at home neither in the human nor in the canine world.

Sirius is the creation of Thomas Trelone, a scientist who develops a method for stimulating brain growth in unborn animals through the injection of a hormone into their mothers. His research leads to the production of a series of "super-sheep-dogs," and through chance one dog, Sirius, proves so much superior to all the rest that he is raised with Treleone's daughter Plaxy, taught to speak and read, and treated at home with the respect due an intelligence comparable to man's. When he is older he is exposed to a variety of environments and experiences: he herds sheep on a farm in Wales, helps Trelone with his research at Cambridge, and lives for a time with a minister in a slum area of London. Throughout these years he begins to be aware of a split between what he calls his "wolf-nature" or instinctive, lower self, and his "human" or spiritual side. In his wolf-mood he can see man only as a repulsive tyrant with "the uncouth hairless features of a super-ape" (229); fearing and despising mankind, he reverts to bestiality and kills a ram and later a pony. In the truly "human" mood, however, he desires what Stapledon's most awakened characters always seek: he wants to play a role in the quickening of the spirit, in whatever form it may manifest itself. After Trelone dies, Sirius enters into a kind of spiritual symbiosis with Plaxy; but the relationship is impaired by the hostility of the villagers, and it is broken up altogether when Plaxy is drafted into the national service during World War II. Left alone, Sirius turns wild and is killed.

Perhaps the most complex aspect of Sirius's life is his relationship with Plaxy. Believing that "the most valuable social relationships were those between minds as different from one another as possible yet capable of mutual sympathy" (175), Thomas Trelone raises Plaxy and Sirius as equals but respects their essential differences. The symbiotic nature of their bond is apparent even in childhood, when "Plaxy's hands [are] held almost as common property" in recognition of Sirius's lack of hands (178). The relationship is strained by their awakening sexual interest in others of their own species, by long periods of enforced separation, and by the dog's growing disenchantment with the entire human race. Coming at a time of unusual tension between Sirius and Plaxy, the killing of the pony epitomizes Sirius's rebellion against the world of man, but when the conflict comes into the open both Sirius and Plaxy become more candid about their relationship:

Sirius on his side told her of the conflict which was racking him, the alternating moods of respect and loathing for humanity. "You, for instance, are sometimes the dearest of all things in the world, and sometimes just a horrible monkey that has cast a filthy spell on me." She answered at once, "And *you* are sometimes just my father's experimental dog that I have somehow got tangled up with and responsible for, because of *him*; but sometimes you are—*Sirius,* the part of Sirius-Plaxy that I love." (232)

The two come more and more to think of themselves as Sirius-Plaxy, "a bright gem of community" (268) whose value derives from their love for one another.[18] There are suggestions that that love takes the form of sexual relations between Sirius and Plaxy, although Brunet errs in assuring us that "the text states that their intercourse is a fact."[19] There are many sexual overtones to the relationship, such as Sirius's tendency to refer to Plaxy as his "human bitch," but the passage Brunet cites is somewhat ambiguous: speaking to the narrator (her future husband, Robert), Plaxy says "No, dear Robert, you don't understand. Humanly I do love you very much, but . . . super-humanly, in the spirit, but therefore in the flesh also, I love my other dear, my strange darling" (296). Perhaps stronger evidence of a sexual bond can be found in Robert's "imagining with horror how a beast had awkwardly mauled the sweet human form that I now so fittingly embraced" (297), or in the following passage: "At a later date both Plaxy and Sirius told me much about their life together at this time; but though after our marriage she urged me to publish all the facts for the light they throw on Sirius, consideration for her feelings and respect for the conventions of contemporary society force me to be reticent" (294).

The implication of sexual relations in this last passage is all the stronger because of its similarity to a passage in *Odd John* where the narrator reveals—while pretending to refuse to reveal—that at one point John engaged in an incestuous relationship with his mother, thereby violating "one of the most cherished of all the taboos of [the human] species" (53). John, however, breaks the incest taboo for the sake of breaking it—because "he needed to assert his moral independence of *Homo sapiens,* to free himself of all deep unconscious acquiescence in the conventions of the species that had nurtured him"—while Sirius's action, although obviously a violation of man's moral code, must be seen quite simply as the physical embodiment of a spiritual bond that is essential to the sanity of this quasi-human dog. The relationship of Sirius and Plaxy is thus more logically compared to the love relationships that form the basis for John's colony than to John's incestuous relations with his mother. The community established between Sirius and Plaxy proves much more fragile than the community of supernormals in *Odd John,* however, for it is flawed by their different perceptions of the "human" condition and it is threatened by the fears and superstitions of other people from the beginning of their "marriage." Stapledon may be glancing at racial attitudes here, but the full force of his argument can be felt only if we see that he is asking us to disregard appearances altogether and to focus on the spirit. The sexual theme in *Sirius* can best be understood as an extreme example of a recurrent motif in Stapledon's works: again and again we see individuals who appear homely or even grotesque or deformed to the "unawakened" eye, but whose true beauty becomes apparent to our awakened selves.

Stapledon, however, would be the last to deny a connection between the physical and spiritual aspects of being: Sirius's spiritual development, after all, is hampered by his lack of hands and his poor vision, but it is advanced by the keen perception of odors and sounds that makes him sensitive to realms of experience to which Plaxy is a stranger. The name Sirius, suggesting the Dog Star, may itself imply a duality of subhuman and superhuman, canine body and celestial spirit; only at the end of the novel, when he dies and "the sun's bright finger set[s] fire to Sirius," can we view Sirius as pure flame or spirit. Meanwhile, Sirius's passion for the spirit manifests itself most clearly in his relationship with Plaxy and in his "singing," an odd form of music reminiscent of James Jones's playing in *Odd John*. In perhaps the most memorable scene in the novel, Sirius sings at a church service conducted by the Reverend Geoffrey Adams, a sympathetic pastor. His song, which Reverend Adams terms "a very lovely miracle," gives the parishioners a chance to view the struggle of man's spirit from a nonhuman perspective; but unlike the vision of the stars that John gives the two mountain climbers, this "vision" is comprehensible to very few who experience it: "To most of the congregation it was an inconsequent mixture of music and noise, and moreover a mixture of the recognizably, comfortably pious and the diabolical" (260). Like Nietzsche's Zarathustra, who is misunderstood when he speaks of the superman, Sirius finds that his great song falls on deaf ears.

The Moral Dimension

The similarities between *Odd John* and *Sirius* are so striking that it is difficult not to view the two books as companion pieces. The central metaphor of *Sirius* is borrowed (in inverted form) from the earlier novel, where John continually sees human beings as dogs: he refers to Constable Smithson as an "amiable bloodhound" (32), and when he is commencing sexual relations with a beautiful young woman he suddenly feels "as though a dog were smelling round me, or a

monkey" (52). The narrator, whom John likes to call Fido, uses
similar terms: he describes the mixed ethnic heritages of John's parents
by saying that Pax "was no less a mongrel than her husband" (7), and
when John ironically quotes Hegel in a conversation with a capitalist,
he says that "like a dog encountering an unfamiliar and rather
formidable smell, Mr. Magnate sniffed this remark, bristled, and
vaguely growled" (22). In a broader sense, the pattern of the two
books is the same: John's late physical development, his rejection both
of orthodox religion and of pure materialism, and his awakening
devotion to the spirit are all reproduced in the life of Sirius. Specific
incidents also suggest a close parallel between John and Sirius. Thus
John is first knocked down by a larger boy named Stephen, then
teaches himself to fight, lures Stephen into a fight, and defeats him
soundly. In *Sirius,* the same chain of events occurs, this time involving
Sirius and a larger dog named Diawl Du (Black Devil). Both battles
end in victories for the superhuman over the subhuman, for mind or
spirit over brute instinct, and both presage the greater conflicts to
come.

Other parallels between the two novels suggest contrasts as well as
similarities. When Sirius kills the sheep and the pony, for example, his
action is structurally parallel to John's killing of the deer, but the
motives in the two cases are quite different from each other. The
slaying of the great stag is the act of a superman who reverts to
primitive conditions in order to triumph over the subhuman element
in his own nature. John's attitude toward the stag is complex, for he
sees something of himself in the animal: "With my soul I saluted
him. Then I pitied him, because he was doomed, and in the prime.
But I remembered that I too was doomed. I suddenly knew that I
should never reach my prime" (80). Seeing his own death in the
stag's, John nevertheless kills him, thereby signifying his acceptance of
his own condition. In the case of Sirius, however, almost the reverse is
true. Sirius kills the ram because "it was man's creature, and it
epitomized all the tyranny of the sheep-dog's servitude" (227); that
is, he kills him to symbolize his rejection of the human world. The
murders of the sheep and the pony both demonstrate the increasing
strain caused by Sirius's failure to fit into the human world. Thus,
while John's act helps him to resolve the conflicts in his nature, Sirius

can only respond with an action that aggravates the strife between his "wolf-nature" and his more "human" side.

Perhaps a stronger contrast can be drawn between the attitudes of John and Sirius toward the murder of human beings. For his part, John is directly responsible for the deaths of several innocent persons: first Smithson, the constable who catches him in the act of burglary; then two survivors of a shipwreck whose curiosity about John, the other supernormal children, and their boat causes John to fear the discovery and destruction of his plans to create a colony; and later still the primitive people who have the misfortune to occupy the island selected for the colony. The colonists even conspire in the murder of a Polynesian girl as part of an experiment in eugenics. The narrator is "convinced that John was far superior to the rest of us in moral sensibility" (47), but he remains deeply troubled. John, meanwhile, rests his defense on his superiority, and the superiority of his mission, over man and his society:

"Had we been members of your species, concerned only with the dreamlike purposes of the normal mind, what we did would have been a crime. For to-day the chief lesson which your species has to learn is that it is far better to die, far better to sacrifice even the loftiest of all 'sapient' purposes, than to kill beings of one's own mental order. But just as you kill wolves and tigers so that the far brighter spirits of men may flourish, so we killed those unfortunate creatures that we had rescued. Innocent as they were, they were dangerous. Unwittingly they threatened the noblest practical venture that has yet occurred on this planet." (121)

The distinction between "beings of one's own mental order" and beings of a lower order reappears in *Sirius*. When Sirius mates with another sheep dog, the products of the union are, from his point of view, worse than morons; and since he regards them as examples of an inferior species, he has no qualms about drowning some of them and selling others—that is, treating them exactly as a human being would have. On the other hand, at one point Sirius is put in the care of a particularly brutal farmer, Thwaites, whose "great cruel hands symbolized for [Sirius] the process by which the ruthless species had mastered all the living creatures of the planet" (263–64). When Thwaites strikes another dog Sirius knocks him down; Thwaites responds by getting a gun to destroy Sirius, and Sirius attacks and kills Thwaites, partly in self-defense but also in the insane belief that "In his symbolic act he would kill not only Thwaites but the whole tyrant race. Henceforth all beasts and birds should live naturally, and the planet's natural order should never again be disturbed by the machinations of this upstart species" (264). Yet when the battle is over and he is able to regard the issue more dispassionately, he comes to see himself as a Cain who has murdered his brother; and in a gesture that reveals the ambivalent nature of his feelings toward mankind, he licks "the forehead of his slaughtered brother" (265).

It seems likely that in writing this episode in 1944, Stapledon was thinking about the war that was still to rage in Europe for another year. Stapledon's abandonment of pacifism for the duration of World War II meant that like Sirius, he "realized that the war had to be won, otherwise all that was best in the tyrant species would be destroyed" (273). The danger was that in the process of defeating the Nazis we might become so spiritually damaged that we will be incapable of building a more awakened society after the war. What is necessary is the recognition of our common humanity, just as Sirius recognizes that in some fundamental way he and Thwaites are manifestations of the universal spirit.

The example of the Nazis may well have caused Stapledon to reconsider some of the ideas advanced in *Odd John*. John's adaptation of the Nietzschean idea that the superman is above the moral code of *Homo sapiens* looks very different when it is seen against the background of Hitler's use of the same idea for his own perverse reasons. As William L. Shirer has noted, "no one who lived in the Third Reich could have failed to be impressed by Nietzsche's influence on it," and "in the end Hitler considered himself the superman of Nietzsche's prophecy."[20] In particular, Hitler adopted from Nietzsche the idea that "the supreme leader is above the morals of ordinary man":

A genius with a mission was above the law; he could not be bound by "bourgeois" morals. Thus, when his time for action came, Hitler could justify the most ruthless and cold-blooded deeds, the suppression of personal freedom, the brutal practice of slave labor, the depravities of the concentration camp, the massacre of his own followers in June 1934, the killing of war prisoners and the mass slaughter of the Jews.[21]

Stapledon was coming to realize how easily the most "awakened" ideas could be warped into a new and more stifling orthodoxy. In *Odd John* there is no one capable of contesting John's political ideas, and the confidence with which he advances them reflects Stapledon's own assuredness. Writing about this period, Sam Moskowitz has commented that "Stapledon the philosopher is somewhat cocky, somewhat sure of himself. It is 1934 and everything is in a deplorable state. . . . His patient is the world and he precisely and confidently diagnoses its illnesses and cures."[22] In contrast, *Sirius* reflects its author's growing awareness of his own fallibility. The debate in Stapledon's mind appears in the book as a political debate between Sirius and Plaxy (274–75), in which Plaxy argues that "the people" must plan a better society while Sirius contends that planning should be left in the hands of the "wide-awake people." To Plaxy's argument that "that's the way straight to Fascism. There's a leader who *knows,* and the rest do what they're told. And there's a Party of faithful sheep-dogs who make them do it," Sirius replies that "a Fascist Party is *not* made up of wide-awake people"; but the riposte is not altogether convincing, and it is unlikely that it was meant to be. As Stapledon demonstrates in the depiction of the "mad worlds" in *Star Maker,* the line between the awakening of the spirit and its perversion is razor thin.

Sirius himself moves from one side of the line to the other after Plaxy is forced to leave him to complete her national service during the war. A series of events precipitated by a delusional girl who claims that Sirius raped her forces him into progressively open and violent conflict with the villagers, a conflict that culminates in vigilante action when it is discovered that Sirius has killed and half-eaten a man. Half-mad, he returns to his senses when Plaxy reappears but realizes that "There is no place for me in man's world, and there is no other world for me. There is no place for me anywhere in the universe" (306).

Sirius's ambition has been to be "the hound of the spirit" (248), that is, a sort of prophet who will help to awaken mankind generally into a higher state of spiritual awareness. That this ambition never develops into a practical policy comparable to John Wainwright's founding of the colony is due partly to Sirius's greater isolation—John, after all, has peers while Sirius is unique—and partly to the deep and unresolved divisions in his nature. Still, his nature is ours regarded from another perspective, and if Sirius fails to resolve the conflict of spirit and world, superhuman and subhuman, in the way John does, we find him a more sympathetic character—and a more *human* one— partly because of his strange, tragic love for Plaxy and partly because of his failure to transcend his condition. As Barbara Bengels has observed, "in leaving humanity behind, John has left us behind. In being driven to bestiality, Sirius has nevertheless achieved a kindred humanity for he is the beast—and the man—in us all."[23] In an odd and rather ironic fashion *Sirius,* as its punning title implies, is one of the most *serious*—and certainly one of the most moving—of Stapledon's novels.

Chapter Four

Divine Tragedy

A Cosmic Baedeker

Brian Aldiss contends that "*Star Maker* stands on that very remote shelf of books which contains huge foolhardy endeavours, carried out according to their authors' ambitions: Hardy's *Dynasts* stands there, the writings of Sir Thomas Browne, C. M. Doughty's epic poems, and maybe Milton's *Paradise Lost*."[1] In recent years, *Star Maker* (1937) has also come to occupy a space alongside other largely unread masterpieces. Like some other volumes in this class—Joyce's *Finnegans Wake* and Pound's *Cantos* are prime examples—*Star Maker* suffers from its somewhat exaggerated reputation for difficulty and is sometimes judged obscure because it does not give readers the sort of comfortable and familiar experience they often expect. Yet while *Star Maker* is certainly an unusual science fiction novel, the basic pattern of the book is an old and familiar one: the narrator journeys to other places (and other times), and his physical journey is a metaphor for the inner journey of discovery.

In a sense, there are two main classes of travel novels, one in the line of Daniel Defoe (*Robinson Crusoe*, 1719), the other in the line of Jonathan Swift (*Gulliver's Travels*, 1726). In Defoe's novel, Crusoe, shipwrecked on an island, transforms it into a sort of utopia that reflects all the values he has brought with him to the island; meanwhile, he himself remains fundamentally unchanged throughout the novel. The same pattern holds in Jules Verne's *The Mysterious Island*, in which several Americans are stranded on a South Pacific island where, because of their high character and technological ingenuity, they are able to create an ideal community. On the other hand, in the Swiftian line of travel novels it is the traveler rather than the island that is transformed, so that Gulliver returns from his travels with a radically altered vision of man and society. In much the same way, Prendick returns to London at the end of H. G. Wells's *The*

75

Island of Dr. Moreau and discovers that he can no longer see people simply as people: his experiences with the beast-men of Moreau's island have made him see all men and women as capable of reverting at any moment to their essentially bestial character.

Like Wells's story and like such later science fiction novels as Pierre Boulle's *Planet of the Apes* and Ursula K. LeGuin's *The Left Hand of Darkness*, *Star Maker* may be viewed as a product of the tradition of Swift, for Stapledon's narrator is an ordinary Englishman who undergoes an extraordinary adventure and returns drastically changed. The novel begins with the "I" of the book (he never names himself) sitting on a hillside at night and contemplating his life, his marriage, and the world. His sense of the "futility" and "unreality" of his life and his concern with "the world's delerium" lead him to pose fundamental questions about man's relation to the cosmos. In this state of mind the narrator feels himself leaving his body and beginning a mental journey through space and time as a "disembodied, wandering viewpoint" (29).[2] He travels first to a planet known as "the Other Earth" (because of its similarity to our world), finding there that he is able to enter into the minds of the inhabitants much as the Last Men can enter into the minds of Paul and other First Men. Later he travels to increasingly alien worlds with strange forms of intelligent life. As he goes along, he is joined by various alien mentalities, and together they form a cosmic mind which, in "the supreme moment of the cosmos" (223), sees clearly the nature of the Star Maker, the Prime Mover of the universe. From this high point in his journey, the "I" returns to Earth to face the problems of terrestrial existence fortified by the insight he has gained through his experience.

Star Maker most clearly recalls another famous journey, the travels of Dante Alighieri through the worlds of Hell, Purgatory, and Paradise in the three books of his *Divine Comedy*. The darkness and confusion in the narrator's mind at the beginning of the novel suggest the opening of the *Inferno*, where Dante finds himself lost in a dark wood midway through his life. Stapledon puts it in his own terms:

One night when I had tasted bitterness I went out on to the hill. Dark heather checked my feet. Below marched the suburban street lamps. Windows, their curtains drawn, were shut eyes, inwardly watching the lives of dreams. Beyond the sea's level darkness a lighthouse pulsed. Overhead, obscurity. (11)

Like Dante, Stapledon's narrator will move from the dark world of his soul to an all-encompassing vision of the universe and its creator. On the way he will not be guided by Virgil and Beatrice, but as he eventually discovers, his journey is directed by an advanced race on a distant planet; the various worlds he visits correspond roughly to the different parts of the three afterworlds visited by Dante. Yet as Robert Scholes has observed, the final vision of *Star Maker* is radically different from that of *The Divine Comedy*: "as Dante's vision was essentially comic because God cared for man, so Stapledon's is ultimately tragic, because the Star Maker cares only for creation and the critical contemplation of his creatures."[3] It would be equally accurate to say that while Dante's vision is firmly rooted in the Christian concept of good and evil as absolute values, Stapledon adopts a more complex and morally ambiguous view of the force behind the cosmos: as we learn, the Star Maker transcends the categories of good and evil. The narrator, trapped by the limitations of his individual perspective, tries at first to understand the Star Maker as an embodiment of good or evil, but as other cosmic explorers join the quest, we come to see the Star Maker in altogether different terms.

The Other Earth

As in *Last and First Men*, where the First Men are given a disproportionate amount of attention, the extraterrestrial race subjected to the closest examination in *Star Maker* is the one most like us. The "Other Earth," populated by "Other Men," provides Stapledon with an opportunity to exercise his satiric talents, for much of this section is a caricature of human behavior and man's institutions. At the same time, Stapledon's ability to create a coherent picture of a wholly new race shines forth here, as it does throughout *Last and First Men*. Stapledon bases much of his portrait of the Other Men on a simple biological distinction between mankind and the other mankind. In the process he shows us that to a large extent our view of the world is determined by our biological makeup.

The major biological differences lie in the senses of sight, hearing,

taste, and smell. Compared to us, the Other Men are deficient in two
respects: they are not very sensitive to color, and they are tone deaf.
As a result of the latter defect, "Music . . . never developed in this
world" (38). But their senses of smell and taste are far more
developed—and consequently more important—than ours: they taste
with their hands, feet, and genitals as well as with their mouths, and
every facet of their civilization is affected by the fact that their senses
of taste and smell are more discriminating than their vision or hearing.
The narrator observes, for instance, that while our language includes
many words that originally had to do simply with vision, the pattern is
quite different on the Other Earth: "our 'brilliant', as applied to
persons or ideas, they would translate by a word whose literal meaning
was 'tasty' " (39).

This emphasis on taste inevitably colors (or, we should say, flavors)
their concept of God, who is imagined as having a particularly
delectable taste. Yet there is little agreement about what that taste is:

Religious wars had been waged to decide whether [God] was in the main
sweet or salt, or whether his preponderent flavour was one of the many
gustatory characters which my own race cannot conceive. Some teachers
insisted that only the feet could taste him, others only the hands or the
mouth, others that he could be experienced only in the subtle complex of
gustatory flavours known as the immaculate union, which was a sensual, and
mainly sexual, ecstasy induced by contemplation of intercourse with the deity.
(51)

Besides travestying religious quarrels on Earth, this passage satirizes
the anthropomorphism of terrestrial religions: while we tend to see
God in our own image, the Other Men imagine that God shares their
taste. Quarrels about religion, then, have their basis partly in "race,"
for racial distinctions among the Other Men are "almost entirely
differences of taste and smell" (39). Stapledon develops this relatively
simple concept into a clever satire on racial discrimination, class
systems, and social snobbery. For instance, industrialization has
produced a proletarian class, a "pariah race" whose taste and smell
offend more fortunate people. Their inability to tolerate the pariahs is,
the narrator says, an indication of "the secret guilt and fear and hate
which the oppressors felt for the oppressed" (41), and it is clear that

his commentary is meant to reflect on the relation of social classes on our planet as well.

The satire takes another turn when we are told that many people use deodorants and dègustatants to substitute a more fashionable or pleasing odor and taste for their natural flavor. There is, however, a catch:

Unfortunately, though the taste of the limbs could be fairly well disguised, no effective means had been found for changing the flavour of copulation. Consequently newly married couples were apt to make the most shattering discoveries about one another on the wedding night. Since in the great majority of unions neither party had the orthodox flavour, both were willing to pretend to the world that all was well. (40)

In a novel whose central theme (discussed later in this chapter) is symbiosis and community, such an example of marriages based on hypocrisy and deceit is particularly devastating. As for the Other Men, their society is "rotten with neuroses bred out of these secret tragedies of marriage," and there is little hope that they will discard the class system that produces such a neurotic civilization.

Like us, the Other Men have their communists and fascists, liberals and conservatives. They also have radio and television, which transmit smells and tastes as well as sounds and images. Much like the "feelies" of *Brave New World,* however, radio is intended partly to help control the populace. By directly stimulating a person's brain with a "sexual receiving set," a broadcaster can give him a perfectly simulated experience of sexual union. When the same idea is applied to other areas like dining and sports, politicians realize that they can use the invention to maintain power: "Slum-conditions could be tolerated if there was an unfailing supply of illusory luxury" (45).[4] The invention is taken a step further when scientists make it possible for some people to spend their lives in bed experiencing simulated life through radio programs. At first it appears that Stapledon might be planning simply to inveigh against the disastrous consequences of living a passive life in a totally artificial technological environment—something in the manner of Wells's *The Time Machine* or E. M. Forster's "The Machine Stops"—but his real attack here is in another direction: while religious people, nationalists, and the "Other Fascists" condemn "radio-bliss" for the wrong reasons, Stapledon asks us to identify with those who object that radio-bliss retards "the creation of a world-wide community of awakened and intelligently creative persons, related by mutual insight and respect, and by the common task of fulfilling the potentiality of the human spirit" (48). In a sense, then, the real trouble with radio-bliss is that this technological advance comes at a time when the Other Men are too immature to handle it, and it therefore endangers their spiritual development. The combination of spiritual immaturity and technological sophistication, along with the emphasis on bigotry and the satire on unchecked capitalism, suggests again that this part of *Star Maker* has much in common with the "First Men" sections of *Last and First Men*.

Another link with the earlier novel is that the Other Men are "subject to strange and long-drawn-out fluctuations of nature, fluctuations which [last] for some twenty thousand years" (55); the cyclic rise and fall of their civilization recalls the history of man as he struggles to develop his society only to be set back repeatedly by unforeseen dangers, either from within himself or from outside Earth.[5] On a larger scale, these cycles suggest the pattern of cosmic creation that the narrator later envisions: the Star Maker creates a series of cosmoses, allowing each to reach its potential and run down before being superseded by another. Here, the narrator sees the futile struggle of the Other Men toward awakening, and their constant slide backward into barbarism, as evidence that "Hate must be the Star Maker" (61); but Bvalltu, an Other Man with whom he has made contact, regards the issue more dispassionately and argues that even a tormented existence deserves praise. Like the Last Men, Bvalltu is able to rise above his own condition and adopt a more cosmic perspective on the nature of human life. But that is not enough: to learn more, the narrator must travel again.

Political and Social Satire

Although it is many other things as well, *Star Maker* is partly a satire on the mental errors that plague human culture and prevent the "awakening" that Stapledon always sought. The satire is particularly obvious in the Other Earth section, perhaps because that is the most conventional part of the book and therefore the part where it is easiest to suggest an analogy with terrestrial institutions, but the satiric element surfaces in other places as well. A brief example is the description of a world where a "cult of irrationalism" takes over (87–88). People begin to admire "brute-men," and despotic and brutish leaders rise to power in many countries; meanwhile, women so desire to have children fathered by these men that they willingly pay to be fertilized by them, either through artificial insemination or through intercourse. It is bad enough that the business becomes commercialized in the "democratic" countries, but in totalitarian societies the situation is even worse. There, "a tyrant of the fashionable type gathered upon his own person the adoration of the whole population. He was the god-sent hero. He was himself divine. Every woman longed passionately to have him, if not as a lover, at least as father of her children." In some places the leader "condescended to be the father of the whole future population" through artificial insemination. The results are catastrophic: the level of intelligence among the populace declines drastically, the race descends to the level of barbarism, and eventually the people are exterminated by a "rat-like animal" which they are no longer intelligent enough to defend against.

On its more obvious level, this section may be read as a warning against allowing the irrational element in all of us to dominate our culture. In this sense, the brute-men, who are roughly equivalent to Swift's Yahoos, represent exactly what they are: they personify the anti-intellectual, subhuman element in man's culture, the most obviously destructive aspect of what, in *Last Men in London*, Stapledon calls our "simian" nature. But it is on the level of contemporary history that this section is most effective, for the rise of the brute-men is an allegory for the rise of fascism in Europe and of the "mob mentality" elsewhere in the 1930s. In particular, the swaggering figure of the "mob-controller" who is worshipped by his half-crazed followers suggests Mussolini or Hitler, while the use of artificial insemination to produce a more brutelike race parodies Nazi attempts to "purify" their race.[6] (Since official Nazi propaganda depicted the Slavs, Jews, and some other "non-Aryan" groups as subhuman, part of the satire here derives from treating the Nazis themselves as subhuman.) More broadly, in dealing with the possibility of a fatal decline in human mentality, Stapledon is returning to a theme that appears in

several of his other works. The destruction of the brute-men's culture
by rats, in fact, anticipates one of the two possible ends of the human
race outlined in Stapledon's next novel, *Darkness and the Light*. Here,
as in that book, the end of the race is appropriate, for the rats
represent the element of self-destructive bestiality that becomes intri-
cately woven into the fabric of the race.

A more elaborate reference to fascism appears in a later part of the
novel, where Stapledon describes the rise of "mad" or "perverted"
worlds. These are fairly advanced, even "awakened," worlds that
become obsessed with interstellar travel. Filled with "missionary zeal,"
they insist on converting other races, and when they are rebuffed they
try to destroy the other worlds. Eventually a "League" is formed to
resist the "United Empires" of the mad worlds, but the sane worlds
find themselves at a disadvantage because their democratic systems
make them far less efficient than the military dictatorships they face.
More effective, for a while, are some highly developed pacifistic worlds
that use telepathic hypnosis to destroy the "communal mind" or group
mentality of the invaders. Unfortunately, the result is that the United
Empires decide that "certain seemingly pacifistic worlds [are] in fact
more dangerous than all other enemies" (161) and determine to
destroy them by causing their suns to explode. After three such
disasters, however, an even more developed race uses its telepathic
powers on the United Empires. The narrator describes the nature of
this power:

It could dispense with the aid of normal intercourse, and it could overcome
every resistance. It could reach right down to the buried chrysalis of the spirit
even in the most perverted individual. This was not a merely destructive
power, blotting out the communal mind hypnotically; it was a kindling, an
awakening power, brought to bear on the sane but dormant core of each
individual. (170–71)

The result is a triumph, but a mixed one, for while many of the mad
worlds are transformed into truly awakened races, others descend to
barbarism or commit suicide.

This sequence may be interpreted in a number of ways. At heart, it
is an attack on what, in *Waking World,* Stapledon calls "the
mechanic's mentality."[7] Since Stapledon criticized Russia as well as

the capitalistic countries for "sacrificing at the mechanic's shrine," Curtis Smith is undoubtedly right to suggest that in the mad world episode "Stapledon is satirizing what he conceives to be the U.S.S.R.'s mania for industrial development to the exclusion of the quality of life."[8] But the references here point more directly to the menace of fascism than to the flaws in the Russian system: the failure of the League to stop the mad worlds, for example, suggests the inability of the League of Nations to cope with the expansionist policies of Japan, Italy, and Germany in the 1930s. The defeat of the pacifistic worlds, on the other hand, does not indicate that Stapledon was abandoning his allegiance to pacifism, only that he realized that pacifism alone would not stop the march of a Hitler. What is needed, he seems to say, is a genuine transformation of the spirit, something he is able to produce here only through the *deus ex machina* intervention of a race with advanced telepathic powers.

Perhaps the most ingenious and most successful political and social satire in *Star Maker* may be found in the description of the world of the Nautiloids, mollusc-like beings that evolve into something very close to the shape of a ship. Taking a page out of Wells's *The Time Machine,* Stapledon describes "the splitting of the population into two mutually unintelligible castes through the influence of economic forces" (93). The two classes here are radically different, both physically (the masters are delicate, like Wells's Eloi, and the workers like the Morlocks are hardy) and mentally (the masters tend to be "prudent, far-seeing, independent, self-reliant" while the workers are generally more altruistic and less individualistic [94]). Yet social class in this world is determined not by parentage but by what side of the mother one is born on:

After weaning, all children born on the port side of the mother, no matter what the parental caste, were brought up to be members of the master caste; all those born on the starboard side were brought up to be workers. Since the master class had, of course, to be much smaller than the working class, this system gave an immense superfluity of potential masters. The difficulty was overcome as follows. The starboard-born children of workers and the port-born children of masters were brought up by their own respective parents; but the port-born, potentially aristocratic children of workers were mostly disposed of by infant sacrifice. (94)

From this premise, Stapledon develops a sophisticated and ironic commentary on the "nature-nurture" controversy, the argument over whether heredity or environment is the more important determinant of intelligence and personality. In a development reminiscent of Mark Twain's *Pudd'nhead Wilson*,[9] some port-born (master class) infants are brought up as members of the working class and become in every respect like the workers born on the starboard side; this causes capitalists, who see the potential benefits in increasing the number of workers, to develop moral qualms against infanticide. Oddly enough, the industrialists do not seem to foresee the obvious corollary: as scientists soon discover, "starboard-born children brought up as masters developed the fine lines, the great sails, the delicate constitution, the aristocratic mentality of the master caste" (95). The result of these discoveries is that the world is split between the forces of revolution and reaction: in one part of the world there is a communist dictatorship that promises a classless society, while in other parts there is fascistic reaction against "materialistic science" and the emergence of a dictator along the lines of Hitler or Mussolini. The struggle of these two forces devastates the civilization of the Nautiloids and reduces them to "almost subhuman savagery," but in time the race rebuilds itself and develops a higher and saner civilization.

Like other sections of *Star Maker*, this one combines satiric commentary with thematic development. In this episode Stapledon takes sides in the nature-nurture argument, showing that environment is actually the sole determinant of the Nautiloids' physical and intellectual development. The section also attacks capitalistic industrialism and argues that the profit motive, if unrestrained, may lead to moral bankruptcy. Finally, the whole sequence is related to the world situation in 1937 through references to the development of communism and fascism and the inevitability of war between these two ideologies. Beyond all of this, however, the episode is thematically significant in quite a different way. Throughout the novel, one of Stapledon's most important themes is "symbiosis" or "community"; building on a foundation of cooperation and respect for one another's individuality, certain races create utopian societies and "awaken" into a higher state of spiritual awareness. A world like that of the Nautiloids, in which the race splits into two subspecies and one exploits the other, is therefore the antithesis of the ideal world of true cultural and spiritual development. This is why the war between the revolutionaries and the reactionaries is unavoidable: the civilization of the Nautiloids is so grossly perverted that it cannot be reformed but must be destroyed and then rebuilt. There is evidence elsewhere in *Star Maker* that Stapledon saw our situation on Earth as more hopeful, but it is undeniable that the Nautiloid episode gives us a very dark view of man's spiritual crisis.

Symbiosis

On the opening page, the narrator of *Star Maker* refers to his relationship with his wife: "I distinguished our own house, our islet in the tumultuous and bitter currents of the world. There, for a decade and a half, we two, so different in quality, had grown in and in to one another, for mutual support and nourishment, in intricate symbiosis" (11). Throughout the book, this symbiotic relationship—described variously as "this indescribable union of ours," "the little jewel of personal union," and at the end, "our little glowing atom of community"—is recalled. Stapledon is thinking of his own marriage to Agnes Miller, but the autobiographical basis of the narrator's marital situation is far less important than the thematic relationship of this marriage to the rest of the novel. Stapledon turns the idea of symbiosis into the central metaphor of the book; in addition, the narrator's vision of the Star Maker is made possible by another kind of symbiotic relationship.

The narrator sees that his marriage is "a microcosm of true community" and "an actual and living example of that high goal which the world seeks" (12). The ultimate example of symbiosis will go far beyond the world, however, for the evolution of the cosmic spirit in quest of self-knowledge is the apotheosis of symbiotic community. Along the way, the theme surfaces in virtually every part of the book, but the clearest instance of it is in the "symbiotic race" of "Ichthyoids" and "Arachnoids." These two distinct species, both of them intelligent, develop on the same planet, with the fishlike Ichthyoids controlling the seas and the crablike Arachnoids ruling dry land. At first they see one another merely as rivals or even as enemies, but later they enter into a partnership that evolves into "biochemical interdependence" (105). At this point a complex pattern of interspecific pairings develops: adolescent Ichthyoids and Arachnoids each take lifelong partners of the other species, and these pairings are to them more important than the sexual matings with members of their own species, necessary for the propagation of each race. Although the symbiotic pairings are primarily mental, they also have sexual overtones since they always involve a male and a female, the male acting "with parental devotion" toward his partner's offspring. More importantly, the relationship of the two species allows them the advantages of specialization without its drawbacks: the Ichthyoids are superior in theoretical, and the Arachnoids in practical, matters, yet the close mental and emotional bonds of the partners allow each to participate in the achievements of the other.

The narrator says that before the planet became mechanized, the two races avoided "the cleavage into masters and economic slaves" because "the communal spirit . . . triumphed over all individualistic enterprise" (107). The communal spirit, however, is threatened when the Arachnoids learn how to produce fire; they quickly put the world through an industrial revolution while their aquatic partners, unable to make use of fire, resent their own increasingly subordinate status. The conflict leads to tension, war, and even attempted genocide before enlightened members of both species are able to reconstruct the symbiotic bond that lies at the heart of the matter. Two later developments ensure the continuation of the relationship: they find a way "to establish full telepathic intercourse between the two members of each couple" and eventually among the whole race, and the brain capacity of the Ichthyoids is increased so much that they can maintain an equal relationship with the Arachnoids despite their limited practical abilities. Now, both species can develop their special talents. The Arachnoids explore space, returning periodically to visit their partners, while the Ichthyoids create "a fixed network of . . . individuals in direct neural connection with one another"—in short, a huge brain consisting of all the Ichthyoids on the planet (166). In so doing, they become the first of the "minded worlds" which together develop into the cosmic spirit.

In some ways the Symbiotics are the most important race in the galaxy. Once they have "awakened," they assist other races in reaching their own level of development, so that they are largely responsible for the growth of the galactic, and then the cosmic, mind. They are also the race that initiates and guides the journey of the narrator and other cosmic explorers, and when the United Empires threaten to destroy saner races, the telepathic powers of the Symbiotics end the menace. As an allegory of human development, the two species suggest man's divided (but potentially unified) nature: the Ichthyoids embody the theoretical, mystical, and introverted aspects of our being, while the Arachnoids represent our practical, rational, extraverted selves. The crisis in their history, when the discovery of fire allows the Arachnoids suddenly to overshadow the Icthyoids, occurs during a time analogous to our present century, a time when man's technological and scientific genius has developed too quickly for him to be able to cope with the fruits of his technology. More broadly, however, the pattern of development of the Symbiotics is a miniature version of the history of the cosmos, as the intelligent life of the universe begins in isolated confusion, reaches out tentatively for other forms of itself, suffers setbacks, and finally breaks through into a lucidity made possible only by cooperative effort.

The communal theme is seen in other terms elsewhere in the book. Some of the complications of the theme are indicated by the portrayal of a society of "Human Echinoderms." In this race there is a struggle between the individual and the group—a struggle in which, because of biological and social factors, the independence of the individual is threatened. The Echinoderms reproduce at certain times when the entire tribe emits a fertilizing "pollen," so that "Every child, though it had an individual as its mother, was fathered by the tribe as a whole" (83). Because children are raised "communally," and because the tribe is the only "lover" the individual Echinoderm ever knows, there is a tendency for individuality to become suffocated by the group. A reaction against this herd-instinct takes the form of a "religion of self," but the religion is unsuccessful because "the precept 'Be true to thyself,' bred the disposition merely to be true to the tribal fashion of mentality" (85). Stapledon may be suggesting the danger of the suppression of individuality in communist and fascist countries, but it is equally important to see that the culture of the Echinoderms is a mirror image of Stapledon's vision of capitalistic societies where each

man respects his own individualism but denies the right of others to be
truly different—as he says, "The precept, 'Love thy neighbour as
thyself,' breeds in us most often the disposition to see one's neighbour
merely as a poor imitation of oneself, and to hate him if he proves
different." Thus the growth of world government would be a valuable
corrective to our selfish individualism, while for the Echinoderms it
poses the threat of complete obliteration of the individual.

The supreme example of communal enterprise may be found in the
growth of the cosmic mind. As he is joined first by Bvalltu and then
by other mental explorers of the universe, the narrator becomes part of
a great mind that can understand much that, by himself, the narrator
could never have understood. Yet this experience—much like the
racial experience of *Last and First Men*—does not obliterate the
individuality of each member of the group:

In one respect, namely unity of consciousness, we were indeed a single
experiencing individual; yet at the same time we were in a very important
and delightful manner distinct from one another. Though there was only the
single, communal 'I', there was also, so to speak, a manifold and variegated
'us', an observed company of very diverse personalities, each of whom
expressed creatively his own unique contribution to the whole enterprise of
cosmical exploration. . . . (134–35)

The same pattern holds, on a wider scale, when "minded worlds" join
in a galactic community. Still later it is discovered that the stars
themselves have a form of intelligence, and after many difficulties "a
symbiotic society of stars and planetary systems embraced the whole
galaxy" (206). And, when the galactic mind makes contact with other
galaxies, the "cosmic mind" emerges. It is this mind that explores its
own past, communicating with the giant nebulae from which the
galaxies developed, and later explores past cosmoses. In the "supreme
moment" of the cosmos, the cosmic mind envisions its creator, the Star
Maker.

This vision is what the book has been pointing toward, and it is in
a sense the *raison d'être* for the theme of symbiosis throughout the
novel. In a practical sense, the vision attained in this book is supposed
to be far beyond the imaginative grasp of any one of the cosmic

explorers, but together they can see something which the English author of the book dimly remembers and writes down in terms that we can understand. But in another sense, the question asked at the beginning of the book is implicit in the whole journey. Is the principle of love and mutual understanding—the symbiotic relationship exemplified by the narrator's marriage—a fundamental law of the universe, something implicit in the created cosmos and therefore reflective of the mind of the Star Maker, or is it perhaps totally insignificant, a sentimental notion unsanctioned by the blind, indifferent cosmos? To put the question another way: will there be anything to see at the end of the journey, and if so, can we praise it? Or, to state it most simply: does our life have meaning in relation to the cosmos?

These are questions that Olaf Stapledon first posed in *Latter-Day Psalms* and struggled with throughout his life. In the vision of the Star Maker, Stapledon proposed an answer.

The Myth of Creation

The truly incredible scope of *Star Maker* becomes apparent only in the latter half of the book. Here, the entire two billion year history of man that is recounted in the three hundred or more pages of *Last and First Men* is reduced to a single paragraph (185). Stapledon widens his lens even further, though, for his vision will eventually encompass not only the entire history of the cosmos—a matter of a few hundred billion years—but *the histories of other cosmoses* as well. The possible existence of sequential universes may take some getting used to, but it is crucial to Stapledon's conception of the Star Maker not as God, in the usual sense, but as the supreme artist, creating successive cosmoses until the ultimate cosmos expresses most perfectly the spirit of its creator. Our whole universe, as it develops, is only a rough draft—and not a particularly good one at that—for the final text of the ultimate cosmos.

As the cosmic mind, the narrator follows the development of "spirit" in the universe. First he makes contact with the giant nebulae, then he races through the history of the galaxies until, long after they have passed their physical prime, the galaxies, and finally the cosmos itself, awaken into a great telepathic community. It is this community that envisions the Star Maker. The narrator sees the Star Maker "in two aspects: as the spirit's particular creative mode that had given rise to me, the cosmos; and also . . . as the eternally achieved perfection of the absolute spirit" (224). The two aspects of the Star Maker's being explain why the Star Maker creates not out of love—or, for that matter, hate—but out of a need to objectify its qualities so as to know its potentiality. The Star Maker, that is, creates for much the same reasons that the cosmos explores itself and "awakens."

The narrator, in his role as the cosmic consciousness, does not of course actually *see* the Star Maker. Rather, he envisions the creator in a dream—a mystical vision that is our nearest possible approach to direct apprehension of the unknowable. In the dream, then, we see the Star Maker first as an "infant" with "unexpressed potency" (236). He creates a "toy cosmos, a temporal rhythm, as it were of sound and silence." After this, each succeeding cosmos is created in response to the Star Maker's experience of the previous ones. They become more complex and, from our point of view, more fantastic: we are asked to imagine universes without space or without time; musical cosmoses; universes in which our laws of gravity and entropy are reversed; and many other strange possiblities. Eventually the Star Maker conceives the divine and satanic aspects of his being and makes them the fundamental principles of a series of cosmoses. In one of these, there are actually three separate universes corresponding to the Christian Earth, Heaven, and Hell; those who are tempted by the Star Maker's "evil" aspect are doomed to eternal pain, while those who resist are rewarded with "an eternal moment . . . of ecstatic comprehension and worship" (243). Later, with Hell overpopulated and Heaven virtually empty, the divine or "good" part of the Star Maker becomes incarnate "to redeem the sinners by his own suffering" (244).

After seeing these earlier cosmoses, the narrator is able to watch the fashioning of our own universe, viewing it "not from within the flux of the cosmical time" but "in the time proper to the Star Maker" (247–48). It is from this perspective that he learns to praise the Star Maker. This urge to praise is one of the most paradoxical qualities of Stapledon's vision in this novel, for the narrator is also somewhat frightened of, and appalled by, the Star Maker's cold indifference to his creation. We praise the Star Maker—but we do not love him. In part, that is because one of the problems that leads the narrator on his journey, and continues to plague him to the end, is how to justify the pain and frustration that are so much a part of our lives and of life elsewhere in the universe. That pain continues—and in a sense is intensified—in cosmoses created after ours, even the "ultimate cosmos." Yet when the final cosmos faces its maker it, too, praises, and out of that praise is conceived the "absolute spirit" or perfect form of the Star Maker which he has striven to create (255). The passage is not easy to follow, but the idea seems to be that pain is a part of the Star Maker's being, much as it is part of any artist, and that in the end—as Pope, working from different premises, found—"Whatever is, is right."[10]

The image of the Star Maker is also paradoxical in that it seems to be both an evolving and an unchanging and perfect spirit. Roger Brunet has commented on this apparent contradiction, arguing that Stapledon's concept of the Star Maker is an attempt to reconcile Aristotelian and Platonic ideas. Since each cosmos is a reflection of the Star Maker's current knowledge of itself, and since the creator seems to change in response to his creations, Stapledon is drawing on "Aristotle's conception of nature or reality as a process of becoming, combined also with Bergson's theory of an *élan vital* where nature . . . evolves towards the perfect." But as Brunet notes, "In the second aspect the Star Maker is eternally perfect" in accordance with Plato's concept of the Absolute.[11] The paradox may be resolved if we observe that the Star Maker stands outside of time as we know it, and that in any case the Star Maker as creator is only one aspect of the eternal and unchanging spirit that it discovers itself to be. The real point, though, is that since these two aspects of the Star Maker simultaneously coexist, so do the two aspects of his creation: the evolving worlds of flux and pain, and the final form of creation in which all is comprehended. In this way, the ultimate creation "redeems" all the others.

Return

In the last part of the book, with the narrator back on Earth, Stapledon turns his attention from his great cosmic theme to the world of 1937. In his imagination he circles the globe, seeing the war in Spain, the rise of fascism, the peoples of Asia, Africa, and America. He regards the world as an arena in which the forces of darkness and light—the "awakened" mentality and "the cunning will for private mastery"—struggle. How, he asks, in the coming battle, can we preserve the "spirit's integrity" in ourselves?

He gives two answers. First, there is love—"our little glowing atom of community." Besides this, there is the "hypercosmical reality" that he has discovered in his search for the Star Maker. He has reached the point where, as Brunet puts it, "loyalty to man and loyalty to fate are one."[12] This is, in a sense, the justification for the book, a book that may initially seem to have no relevance to prewar Europe. Stapledon's argument—advanced first in his preface and reiterated in the last few pages of the book—is that his novel is not "a distraction from the desperately urgent defence of civilization against modern barbarism"; instead, he stresses the need for " 'self-critical self-consciousness of the human species', or the attempt to see man's life as a whole in relation to the rest of things" (7–8). In the end, "the rest of things" comes to include "the cold light of the stars," the light in which, because of its very indifference to us, we gain importance. Stapledon was neither an existentialist nor an absurdist, but the end of *Star Maker* is strikingly like that of Albert Camus's *The Stranger* (1942), where Meursault, condemned to death, lays his "heart open to the benign indifference of the universe" and in so doing finds that he is both free and happy.[13] The difference between Camus and Stapledon—and it is an important one—is that in Stapledon we see that we are not alone; that we are, or could be, part of the great movement and growth of spirit throughout the universe; and that our individual lives are redeemed when we rise out of and beyond ourselves and are absorbed into the whole.

Epilogue: *Nebula Maker*

Among the many papers that remained in Olaf Stapledon's library after his death was a hundred page holograph manuscript bearing the title "Discarded MS. of Star-Maker." Discovered by Harvey Satty, the manuscript was first published in 1976 under the title *Nebula Maker*; today it is available in paperback. Although it is incomplete, *Nebula Maker* deserves study both for the light it sheds on the evolution of *Star Maker* and for its own value as a work of philosophical and speculative fiction.

Near the beginning of *Nebula Maker*, the narrator, feeling

"infuriated, and then utterly cowed, by the insensitiveness and vastness of the cosmos," believes that he sees the "immense and dimly lucent face" of God behind the stars (4–5).[14] Soon, that face undergoes a series of changes that may simply represent the many ways in which men apprehend God; on another level, however, the changes parallel God's creation of a series of cosmoses leading to ours. Soon the narrator finds himself watching the creation of the universe, which is described in a style that parodies Genesis (12–15). The remainder of the novel, to the point where Stapledon abandoned the draft, describes the growth, social organization, mentality, and eventual demise of the great nebulae.

Many differences can be seen between Stapledon's methods here and in *Star Maker*. Stapledon originally planned to take his readers through the universe in chronological order: thus the narrator visits the nebulae, and in later chapters he would have moved to the stars and then the planets. The structure of *Star Maker*, on the other hand, is almost the reverse: instead, the narrator first journeys to the Other Earth and other planets before discovering that the stars and even the nebulae are intelligent beings. Rather than following the evolution of intelligence and spirit in the order in which it occurred, *Star Maker* begins with the forms of intelligence that the reader can most easily comprehend and then moves on to other, more abstractly conceived, intelligences. Technically, then, the plot structure of *Star Maker* is more complex than that of *Nebula Maker*, but the reader finds it easier to suspend his disbelief in the narration if it begins with relatively familiar elements.

Nebula Maker opens with the startling declaration that "I have seen God creating the cosmos, watching its growth, and finally destroying it." Throughout the short novel, Stapledon refers to the maker of the universe as "God," but in the later version the term "Star Maker" enables the author to avoid the orthodox religious terminology that might contradict the agnostic mysticism of his vision. The word "God" has far too many firmly entrenched associations for Stapledon to be able to use the word for his own purposes, but Stapledon is free to make the "Star Maker" into a figure that is neither good nor evil, neither God nor Satan, but simply the narrator's conception of the creative force behind the growth of spirit in the cosmos. In *Star Maker,* indeed, the narrator's realization that the term "God" is inadequate represents a major step toward the final vision of the novel. A further difference between the two versions of the novel may be detected in the narrator himself, for in *Nebula Maker* the terrestrial narrator never relinquishes his individual identity, never joins in a group mind or cosmic mind. The effect of the change in narrative perspective in the later draft is twofold: it supports Stapledon's contention that his narrator is reporting a vision that is too complex for our limited mentalities, and it underscores the theme of community and symbiosis which is a major element in *Star Maker* but not in *Nebula Maker.*

Perhaps the most important, or at least the most obvious, of the differences is that, as Harvey Satty puts it in his introduction to *Nebula Maker,* the nebulae in the original version have "a rich artistic and historical heritage," while in *Star Maker* the nebulae are "rather simpler primitive creatures almost unable to communicate with one another, and having no history" (viii). To put it slightly differently: in *Nebula Maker* the nebulae are anthropomorphized to a great extent, while in *Star Maker* they are seen much more abstractly. It is easy to see that in treating the nebulae as human beings, even to the point of referring to some as "recruiting sergeants" and others as "war-lords," Stapledon was not really trying to depict the nebulae in their own terms but was merely using them to satirize human society. When he rewrote the book and included many societies that were more like man's, he was able to shift some of the satiric elements originally associated with the nebulae into other sections of the novel. Thus, for example, the "Pan-Cosmical League" (83–84), a nebular version of the League of Nations, is transformed in *Star Maker* into the League that is set up to deal with the "mad" worlds.

While most of the revisions are evidence of Stapledon's growing confidence in himself as narrative artist, the reader of *Nebula Maker* cannot help lamenting the deletion of one element from the revised version of *Star Maker.* That element is the portrayal of two exemplary nebulae who represent the saint and the revolutionary: Bright Heart, a pacifist whose life often follows the pattern of Christ's life, and Fire Bolt, a Marxist radical who attempts to inspire a cosmic revolution. The characterization of Bright Heart and Fire Bolt anticipates

Stapledon's description, in *Saints and Revolutionaries* (1939), of these two types of heroic individuals. The saint, he says, is concerned largely with improving man from within: the real revolution, according to the saint, must take place within the minds and hearts of individual people. Thus Bright Heart preaches a gospel of love, self-sacrifice, and pacifism. The revolutionary, however, realizes that "no . . . widespread change of heart can be created by mere exhortation, and that we must begin by changing the structure of society."[15] Accordingly, Fire Bolt argues that the old order must be destroyed by force before a spiritual revolution can succeed. He is persuaded by Bright Heart, however, to postpone action until the saint's methods have been fully tested. When the martyrdom of Bright Heart fails to transform the spirit of the cosmos, Fire Bolt tries his revolutionary tactics, but they too fail.

The point seems to be that while Bright Heart and Fire Bolt each grasp an important part of the truth, neither type of person has a corner on the truth, and neither course of action will succeed by itself. Instead, as Stapledon says in *Saints and Revolutionaries,* the world can be transformed only when the saint is a revolutionary and the revolutionary is a saint.[16] Then, and only then, can we be assured that the social and political environment will reinforce the most "developed" values in each person, and that the human race will be awakened to the life of the spirit.

Chapter Five
Further Worlds of Wonder
Darkness and the Light (1942)

Following the publication of *Star Maker* in 1937, Stapledon's small but enthusiastic corps of readers waited five years before the appearance of his next novel, *Darkness and the Light*. The unusually long interval between novels was due partly to the concentration on social philosophy which resulted in the 1939 publication of three nonfiction works by Stapledon: *Philosophy and Living, New Hope for Britain,* and *Saints and Revolutionaries.* It seems probable, however, that Stapledon's temporary abandonment of fiction and his turn to more overtly serious works were both signs of his growing concern with the bleak world situation. At the end of *Star Maker* Stapledon described a world divided between the "cosmic antagonists" of light and darkness, and certainly the events of the next few years, including Franco's victory in Spain, Chamberlain's capitulation at Munich, the sweep of Nazi forces across Europe, and the stunning Japanese victory at Pearl Harbor, suggested that the struggle of the light against darkness was becoming increasingly desperate.

The seriousness of Stapledon's intentions in *Star Maker* and in *Darkness and the Light* may be gauged by the fact that in the prefaces to both novels he felt compelled to justify his concern with fictional worlds at a time of crisis in the real world. In a sense, the basis of Stapledon's apologia may be traced to *Waking World*, where he argues that "if it is true that the supreme aim of mankind is to perceive and understand and appreciate its world and itself more truly, and to make human society more vital, then we cannot ever afford to neglect the aesthetic activity, since this is . . . one of the most vitalizing and mentally awakening of our activities, and one of the most powerful means of turning the world of to-day into a more human world."[1] That faith in the awakening and humanizing power of literature is implicit in the preface to *Darkness and the Light*, in which after denying that he intends his book to be literally prophetic, Stapledon suggests that the justification for his novel rests on the existence and importance of the conflict that the book describes, and on the power of the "caricature that I have drawn of it . . . to clear the mind and stir the heart" (v).[2] The assumption lying behind the novel—and behind the nonfiction volume *Beyond the "Isms,"* published the same year— is that a military victory over the Germans will not eliminate the causes of the war—nationalism, racial chauvinism, and other aspects of "the will to darkness"—unless it is accompanied by a more enlightened view of ourselves and our function in the world.

Although the ideas advanced in *Darkness and the Light* are of considerable interest as social philosophy, the book's primary aesthetic appeal lies in its form. While it is shorter and less detailed than Stapledon's earlier "future history," *Last and First Men*, and while there are no invasions from Mars, no emigrations to Venus or Neptune, no Great Brains or Flying Men filling its pages, *Darkness and the Light* captures the imagination through a particularly ingenious application of the science fiction device of "alternate time streams" or "alternate universes." Perhaps the best-known example of an alternate universe novel is Philip K. Dick's *The Man in the High Castle* (1962), which received a Hugo Award for its depiction of an America after the Germans and Japanese have defeated the Allies in World War II. Like Dick's novel, whose universe corresponds to our world only until the 1933 attempt to assassinate Franklin D. Roosevelt (an attempt that succeeds in Dick's fictional world), Stapledon's narrator initially sees "the twin streams of history" as "so similar as to be indistinguishable" before they branch out into two separate histories of man's future (2). Following an introductory section that describes the common thread of history before the splitting of our world into two distinct continua, the narrator presents us with separate chronologies of two possible futures. As the title of the book implies, the first of the two parallel worlds described is one in which the "will to darkness" triumphs; in the second, the influence of the "will to light" allows man to overcome great obstacles and to found a Utopian world order.

The point of departure for the alternate futures comes after most of the world has fallen under the control of rival Russian and Chinese empires. Both of these imperialist states are examples of the will to darkness, for both fear and suppress the full development of personality among their subjects. Only in Tibet are an independent and strong-willed people able to avoid the herd-mindedness that afflicts the remainder of the world. At the point where the "dark" and "light" versions of the narrative begin to differ, the empires first try to undermine the Tibetan state by spreading a "synthetic faith" that preaches blind obedience to the state; then they invade Tibet. In the world of "darkness," the invasion succeeds and a subsequent Chinese conquest of Russia results in a world empire, "The Celestial Government of the World." Focusing more on the consolidation of its power over its subjects than on its opportunity to create a richer and more secure life for everyone, the world state becomes increasingly despotic; eventually almost the entire population is surgically fitted with a radio device that not only makes it possible for the government to read everyone's mind but even allows officials direct control over the actions and thoughts of each citizen. But economic catastrophe and a decline in intelligence that makes it impossible for the government to continue to carry out such a complicated operation result in the collapse of the Celestial Government. Reduced to tribal systems, man hangs on to a subsistence-level life-style until in the far future his half-human descendants are attacked and destroyed by rats.

Returning to the invasion of Tibet in his description of the world of "light," the narrator sees the strong spirit of the Tibetan people sustaining them and leading them to a narrow but crucial victory. Various other states assert their independence of the two empires and, with Tibet, create a federation of free states; China, meanwhile, conquers Russia and comes to rule most of the world. In time, the Chinese empire collapses and the Tibetan federation becomes the germ of an enlightened world state. In the world state there are still disputes over such issues as the disposition of American tidal power and the tendency of the bureaucracy to arrogate too much authority to itself, but the peaceful solution of even the most heated arguments is made possible by the good will of all parties and by their recognition of their opponents' sincerity. Yet at a time when the progress of mankind in all spheres is apparently limitless, an announcement by a group of visionary philosophers known as "the forwards" causes a great change. Put briefly, what they claim to have found is that the whole principle of "light" on which their culture is based seems to be undermined throughout the universe by the more widespread, and perhaps fundamental, principle of "darkness." Rather than giving way to nihilism and despair, they propose that man dedicate himself to a great spiritual struggle for a racial awakening that will establish the importance of the spirit as the essential principle of the universe. The experiment fails when a plague nearly destroys the human race, but in the distant future the narrator sees again the rise of mankind, the emergence of still another human civilization after volcanic eruptions change the geography of the entire world, and the remaking of mankind into a higher species whose history the narrator is unable to follow except insofar as he can see that the members of the new species "were loyal to the light and well equipped to serve it, loyal to that same light which my own generation so vaguely sees and falteringly serves" (181).

The narrator of *Darkness and the Light* is a contemporary of Stapledon's whose vision of the future, aided (he believes) by superhuman powers, begins at the moment of his own death. There are obvious practical reasons for adopting this narrator as the vehicle for a dual narrative, but the point of view of the novel is also symbolic in that it suggests that the death of the self—the death, that is, of our perverse concern with our individual wills and destinies—is prerequisite to genuine insight into the life of the spirit. In a state of detached objectivity, unhampered by either the herd-mindedness of the masses or the desire to dominate and control others for his own ends, the narrator is able to observe and report to us the struggle of two forces which he says are latent in each of us today. If it is not a prophecy, *Darkness and the Light* is an allegory of the fluctuation of modern man's heart and mind between two forces that, as we see at the end, are also struggling throughout the universe. The poles of that conflict are stated in the title, perhaps more precisely than is usually recognized: although critics occasionally mistitle the book *The Darkness and the Light* or simply *Darkness and Light*, Stapledon very carefully reserved the definite article for "the light," suggesting that *the light* is something clear and precise but that *darkness*—a kind of spiritual anarchy—lacks definition and meaning except as a negation of the light.

In many ways *Darkness and the Light* recapitulates themes that appear in Stapledon's earlier novels. The opposition of the wills to darkness and the light, for example, is a more broadly stated version of what in *Last Men in London* is called "the conflict between the primitive simian nature and the genuinely human." Stapledon's concern that radio might be used by the government to hold the populace in check appears both in the Other Men's "radio bliss" in *Star Maker* and in the world empire's rule that the common people must be outfitted with radio units so that they can be manipulated by the central government. Likewise, the refusal of the Chinese and Russian empires to allow the more enlightened Tibetans to live in peace is reminiscent of the fate of the Pacific colony in *Odd John*, while the genocidal policy of the conquerors of Tibet in the "dark" version of the future not only suggests Hitler's policy toward the Jews but recalls the extermination of several peoples in *Last and First Men*.

The vision of the "forwards" is also consistent in almost every respect with the agnosticism of Stapledon's earlier works, although it may be presented more bleakly here than elsewhere. Having sought "evidence that man's struggle for the light was in harmony with the essential spirit of the universe," they find only "a vast and obscure confusion of powers, careless not only of man's fate but of all that he had so painfully learned to hold sacred" (162). Thus they come to envision the universe as "no more than a melting snowflake which at any moment may be trampled into the slush by indifferent and brawling titans." In its vision of a universe indifferent to man's values this passage recalls *Star Maker*, although the Star Maker himself is at least a creative spirit while the "brawling titans" of *Darkness and the Light* represent the blind insensitivity of the physical universe to the very concept of spirit. The decision made as a result of this discovery is to sacrifice the entire human race in a desperate attempt to defeat the titans through a massive racial awakening—a project that parallels the attempt of the Last Men to establish the "cosmic ideal," the creation of the "cosmic mind" in *Star Maker*, and the decision of John Wainwright and the other colonists to devote all their energies to producing a "jewel of worship" for the universal spirit. As in

Stapledon's other works, there is a particularly engaging honesty in his refusal to make the unwarranted assumption that man's values are sanctioned by the cosmos, and there is courage in the refusal to convert an agnostic perspective on the universe into a nihilistic or absurdist view of man's dilemma. What counts, in the end, is spirit: as Stapledon says elsewhere, "A living man is worth more than a lifeless galaxy."[3] In this novel, he might well have added that one snowflake of the light is worth a universe of the titans of darkness.

Despite the ingenuity of its narrative framework and the thoroughness with which the alternate futures are developed, however, *Darkness and the Light* may be more satisfying as a philosophical statement than as narrative art. Today, few readers would agree with E. W. Martin's assessment of the book in 1947 as Stapledon's "most readable and unified work to date."[4] Yet it is certainly not the least successful of Stapledon's works, and it deserves attention if for no other reason than that the narrative line provides readers with an unusually clear and direct expression of the relationship between our inner and outer worlds, the life of the spirit and man's political and social life.

Old Man in New World (1944)

Toward the end of *Darkness and the Light*, the narrator watches as mankind remakes itself and the new form of man rapidly passes beyond the understanding of the old. In the novelette *Old Man in New World*, first published separately and later reprinted in the omnibus volume *Worlds of Wonder*,[5] a similar situation occurs. This brief but well-executed tale, which takes place around the end of the twentieth century, focuses on a pageant that celebrates the founding thirty years earlier of the New World Order. The old man of the title, one of the heroes of the revolution, is taken in a two-seater plane from his home to London, where he is an honored guest at the ceremonies. Throughout the first part of the story, the old man and the pilot—a twenty-three-year-old "product of the Revolution"—debate the wisdom of the direction being taken by the world government; in the second part, the old man watches the pageant and, in the end, finds himself moved by the spirit of the ceremony even though intellectually he is convinced that "it was dangerous, and subtly false to the spirit of the Revolution" (281).

As its title indicates, *Old Man in New World* is an allegory, but the "old" and "new" ideas contrasted in the story are by no means as sharply distinguished as "darkness" and "light." Like the "primary" and "secondary" human races at the conclusion of *Darkness and the Light*, both the old man and the young pilot are motivated by the will to light, but because he was raised in the old world the elderly revolutionary has a less fully developed vision of the light than his young companion. Constantly fearing a reversion to prerevolutionary ideas, the old man favors strong social discipline to reinforce the lessons of the revolution. Thus he is disturbed to see what he takes to be the old capitalistic ideals of individualism and false freedom cropping up among the younger generation, and he expresses doubts about the soundness of the new educational policy which is now in its twenty-fifth year.

Unlike the old man, who insists that human nature cannot be altered through the implementation of a new social order and that "society must compensate for our inveterate individualism by a good deal of discipline" (259), the pilot stresses the need for the state to encourage and foster genuine individuality. The argument restates a problem that appears in several of Stapledon's works, most notably *Star Maker*: what sort of balance must be struck between individual freedom and social organization in order to engender personality-in-community? The answer rests firmly on our recognizing that, contrary to what the old man believes, there has been a vast spiritual change in modern man. The change started with the "agnostic mystics" in America and Russia whose world strike averted World War III and led eventually to the abolition of national governments and the establishment of the New World Order. From the young man's point of view (and Stapledon's), the changing social order was merely an external manifestation of the spiritual awakening in all of mankind; once an enlightened government took charge and redesigned the world along socialist lines, the spiritual development of the next generation became easier. The old man, however, remains firmly committed to an outmoded view of mankind in which all changes in humanity must be interpreted in purely social and materialistic terms; thus he contends that "This mystical feeling [of the will to light], as you call it, was just the subjective side of the objective pressure of circumstances,

which forced people to see that they must stand together or perish"
(267).

The old man is concerned with maintaining the order which he
fought to create; the young man is concerned with preventing that
order from stagnating. The new individualism that the pilot and his
peers seek is made possible by the fact that their generation is actually
more responsible, more mature, than the previous one. Obscurely
aware of this curious reversal of roles, the old man imagines the young
people talking to him as if they are "humouring a child that had
suffered and been warped, and would never really grow up" (256).
Ironically, though, the Procession of the Peoples in London features
an innovation which the old man sees as a sign that the young leaders
of the government are themselves too immature to understand the
need for unity and cohesion among all people. The new element in the
parade consists of the introduction of clowns alongside the ranks of
marchers from the former countries of France, Russia, China, Ireland,
and Britain. As representatives of "the undisciplined individuality of
the common man" (276), the comedians burlesque the seriousness of
the pageant and suggest the willingness of the younger generation to
accept criticism, but Stapledon notes that "there was no doubt at all
about their acceptance of the spirit of the whole occasion" (277). In
its contrast between the rigid discipline of the marching columns and
the prankish capering of the jesters, the parade symbolizes the balance
of order and freedom, continuity and innovation, sought by the pilot
and the other members of his generation.

In the climax of the ceremony, a "court fool" sits on the speaker's
platform and mimics the political leaders who address the crowd.
Midway through the President's speech, the Fool steps forward, takes
the microphone, and delivers his own address to the world. Like a
Shakespearean fool who sees with penetrating insight into the absurdity
of the human condition, the Fool begins by reminding us of our
insignificance within the immensity of the universe. Then, as a sort of
raisonneur, he summarizes what Stapledon says in one book after
another: that there is in mankind a will that urges us "To be aware, to
love, to make" (281). That will is of course the will to light, the voice
of the awakening spirit that asserts the value of human life even
against the vastness and meaninglessness of interstellar space. Bound

to his own very limited vision of man, however, the old revolutionary hero can interpret the Fool's spontaneous interruption of the ceremony only as "a cunning bid for popularity" on the part of the President.

Despite its brevity, despite its failure to develop the characters much beyond their symbolic roles, *Old Man in New World* is a surprisingly successful work. The power of the narrative lies partly in its ability to contrast two points of view, and partly in the sympathy with which both attitudes are treated. Caught between two worlds,[6] the old man responds emotionally to the message of the Fool but cannot fit it into the system of thought which carried him through the revolution. His place of honor on the platform is well earned, for without him and others like him there would have been no revolution, no awakening of the spirit of man; yet he is incapable of understanding or fitting into the world that he has helped to create. By developing his story through the perspective of the old man, Stapledon manages both to expose the weakness of the ideas that his character represents and to temper his criticism with understanding and admiration. Despite its status as a minor work, *Old Man in New World* is thus valuable both as a succinct statement of an important part of its author's social philosophy and as a testament to his genuine skill as a literary artist.

Death into Life (1946)

Following the all-encompassing vision of *Star Maker*, Stapledon narrowed his sights in his next three fictional books, focusing first on the two alternate futures of mankind in *Darkness and the Light*, then the more limited vision of man's immediate future in *Old Man in New World*, and finally the life of one intelligent being in *Sirius*. In *Death into Life*, however, Stapledon suddenly reversed directions, producing a work whose scope is almost as ambitious as that of *Star Maker*. In a very general sense, in fact, *Death into Life* seems to be a reworking of *Star Maker*: both books open with an examination of an individual Englishman, move toward a consideration of a racial and then a cosmic spirit, and return at the end to the present situation. The details of the plot, however, reveal a book that is in many ways different from *Star Maker*. We begin by focusing on the rear-gunner in an English bomber over Germany during World War II. When the plane is destroyed by antiaircraft fire, the spirit of the rear-gunner and the spirits of the other crew members "awaken" first into a higher state of individual perception and then, as their distinct identities are annihilated, into a composite spirit. That spirit of the crew is in turn absorbed into the spirit of all who were killed in the war, and in due course the spirit of the war dead is incorporated into the spirit of mankind. Reviewing his past and foreseeing his future, the spirit of man envisions the end of mankind, the growth and eventual death of a cosmic spirit, and even the formation of the universal spirit of all the cosmoses. The book concludes with a close look at the world situation in 1946.

The comparison with *Star Maker* is most strongly suggested by the process through which the rear-gunner is "wakened to be the crew's spirit, and then the spirit of the killed in a certain battle, and then the spirit of Man, and then of this whole cosmos, and then at last the very Spirit herself" (230). Aside from plot details, however, there are at least three major differences between the two novels. The first and most obvious difference is that *Death into Life* is far more abstract and mystical than *Star Maker*, and the mental journey of exploration and discovery, which in *Star Maker* is objectified and externalized in the traveling of the cosmic explorer from one world to another, is here almost entirely internalized. Hence the use of a series of imaginatively conceived worlds to represent aspects of human society is replaced in the later novel by the introspective vision of the spirit of man as he broods over his past and future.

The weakness of this highly internalized narrative is compounded by the second difference, the lack of a clearly defined point of view. Except for a series of autobiographical interludes that adopt the first-person point of view, the book is narrated by a voice that seems to belong to a contemporary man (he speaks of "our times," that is, the postwar era), but nowhere does he explain how he is able to narrate whole sections from the point of view of the spirit of man. Given the precisely defined narrative perspectives of all of Stapledon's earlier books, the vagueness encountered here seems particularly odd. The explanation seems to be that Stapledon was moving toward the purely meditative form of *The Opening of the Eyes* but was not yet prepared to abandon the appearance of traditional narrative structure and point of view. Whatever the cause, however, the effect of the book's abstraction and its ambiguous point of view is that *Death into Life* is one of the most difficult of Stapledon's novels.

The third difference is less a change in narrative technique than an alteration of the final visions of the two books. In *Star Maker* we search constantly for the source of all being, and when we finally encounter it we can conceive it only in anthropomorphic terms, as an artist observing his handiwork with calm, dispassionate, critical attention. Then we watch the successive creation of cosmoses until the ultimate cosmos confronts the Star Maker and "in the mutual joy of the Star Maker and the ultimate cosmos was conceived . . . the absolute spirit itself, in which all times are present and all being is comprised." The "absolute spirit," then, is seen as the product of interaction between creator and creation, not as something immanent in either. In *Death into Life*, the vision stops short of this apocalypse; the "universal spirit," which is the product of all the spirits of all the cosmoses, "yearns for communion with the dark Other, her creator" (225), but all that the spirit of man can see beyond that is the death of the universal spirit.

Two distinctions can be noted here. First, the absolute or essential spirit is created not out of union of the "dark Other" (the Star Maker) and the ultimate cosmos, but out of the cosmoses themselves. Second, the "dark Other" remains unseen, and the narrator admits the possibility that even for the universal spirit the dark Other is "utterly inscrutable and inaccessible." If *Death into Life* is more mystical than *Star Maker*, it is also more agnostic in its abandonment of any form of beatific vision. While vaguely convinced of the existence of the dark Other, the spirit of man must be consoled by the thought that "if the Other is a mere projection of my own desire and fear, still there is the Spirit, the indubitable Spirit; in me, and men, and all the worlds. And to the Spirit I shall be loyal without reserve" (229).

The theme of loyalty to the spirit is developed partly through a series of sketches of individual people whose lives illustrate in various ways the struggle of darkness and the light. The narrator first presents us with capsule analyses of the lives of the crew members and an unnamed "saint" of the city, all of whom are killed in the battle. Then, following the absorption of these distinct spirits into the composite spirit of man, we observe the growth of the spirit of man by examining various "prophets": Gautama Buddha, Socrates, Jesus Christ, Spinoza, Marx, Lenin, and the "false prophet" Hitler. Stapledon uses this brief outline of history to sound once again several of his recurrent themes, including the inadequacy of a purely scientific and materialistic view of reality, the inevitably destructive effects of private wealth under a capitalistic system, and his own ambivalent attitude toward the Bolshevik Revolution and the Communist state in Russia, where ruthlessness casts a pall over the spirit of comradeship. Perhaps most interesting of all is the description of Hitler, which Stapledon converts into an analysis of the spiritual roots of fascism and the war: having shown that the will to light exists in even the most tormented souls, Stapledon argues that in Hitler "the true fire of the spirit was subtly blended with heats of personal resentment against a society that had scorned him" (174–75). The spiritual disease of modern man is so pervasive that the reaction "against the disastrous power of money, and against the falsity of the commercial mind"— the reaction, that is, against the materialistic and self-seeking spirit of the modern age—is warped into the "false religion" of fascism that comes close to destroying the world.

Following its visions of man's future and of other cosmoses, the spirit of man returns to the postwar world to take a second look at various individuals whose spirits are "re-formed for a while within the vastness of the universal Spirit" (230). Like the "I" of *Star Maker* upon his return from his cosmic voyage, the spirits of those killed in the war see themselves and their world in a new light: while they recognize that they were to some extent prisoners of the forces of darkness within them, they also see the significance of their small lives within the giant pattern of the universal spirit. The conflict of wills in all of us is most complexly illustrated by the example of Hitler, whose "little mundane self [is] confronted with a newly awakened, alien self" at his death (234). Following their absorption into the universal spirit and their reemergence as distinct forms, the "mundane self" of the false prophet is able to find salvation in the belief that "My evil, though in me utterly evil, was a needed feature of the whole's form. Someone had to play the part" (235). Such a position is logically consistent with the argument of *Death into Life*, which sees individual people merely as expressions of the spirit of man and finds significance in evil as well as good; but few readers will feel comfortable with the idea that the war was inevitable, and fewer still will be willing to forgive Hitler on the assumption that "Someone had to play the part."

A far more successful feature of the novel is the insertion of several "interludes" in which Stapledon speaks of his married life and relates it to the cosmic themes of the main narrative. In their concern with the minute and particular, these interludes are counterpointed against the large and abstract concepts of the novel as a whole. The thematic relevance of the interludes is always clear, for here as in *Star Maker* Stapledon uses his "symbiotic" relationship with his wife as a microcosm of the growth of spirit everywhere. In a broad sense, too, the pattern of the interludes reproduces that of the novel. The first interlude, "What Is This Dying?" (106), depicts the narrator (Stapledon) and his wife saying good-bye in a subway station. The situation leads him to wonder whether we simply cease to be when we die, or whether we are set free to be absorbed into "some vital and eternal thing." In the second interlude, "The Heart of It" (133–41), Stapledon explores the differences between him and his wife that convert their "indissoluble symbiosis" into a source of "enrichment . . . a welcome participation of each in the uniqueness of the other." The next interlude, "Windows" (177–78), focuses on the way his wife's eyes reveal the soul within them. Throughout these first three interludes, there is emphasis on symbiotic growth as we move from the separated couple at the station toward their clear perception of each other and of their relationship.

The fourth interlude is an excursus into the nature of "Time and Reality" (194–97). The past exists eternally, but Stapledon wonders whether the future "has still to be created" or whether it exists in some sense before it becomes the present. This section, the longest and most complex of the interludes, comes between chapters entitled "The Spirit of Man Considers His Plight" and "Man's Future"; just as the spirit of man has a vision of the future in these chapters, Stapledon remembers that once, long ago, he looked into his wife's eyes and caught a glimpse of the future. The last few interludes return more obviously to the marital theme: "The House without You" (214–15) recalls a three day separation; "The Broken Toy" (226) develops an example of parental love into the hope that love springs "from the heart of the cosmos"; and "Growing Old in Spring-Time" (237–39) depicts man and wife as "ageing gardeners" who begin to feel out of place in springtime. An "End Piece" entitled "Parenthood' (250–51) neatly rounds off the cycle by considering the relationship of Olaf and Agnes Stapledon to their two children, who by 1946 were well into their twenties and no longer dependent on their parents. Products of the union of their parents but increasingly distinct from that union, the children are the link between present and future, and as narrator Stapledon wonders what sort of choices the children will make, and what sort of future there will be for the world. As they age in these last few interludes, the parents' center of interest shifts from themselves to the next generation, much as the rear-gunner and the other crew members abandon their self-centered attitudes at their deaths and replace them with a clearer, more disinterested, perception of themselves and others. In a small way, then, the narrator's recognition that his children must be allowed to "make their alien choices" is a move toward the more cosmic perspective demanded by all of Stapledon's works.

The use of his own marital relationship as a model for the spirit gives *Death into Life* a certain amount of interest for those who would like to see the man behind the works, but it is hardly enough to redeem the entire book. Not many readers would quarrel with Fletcher Pratt's indictment of the novel for its lack of "narrative drive,"[7] for its mysticism makes *Death into Life* the least effective novel that Stapledon published during his lifetime. The drift from philosophical fiction into pure philosophy and the abandonment of imaginable situations were always temptations for Stapledon: his fiction was primarily a vehicle for conveying social and philosophical ideas, and the more abstract the ideas became the more difficult it was for him to find a means of giving them concrete expression. What is important, however, is not simply that *Death into Life* is unsuccessful as a novel, since it was not intended to be a novel in the first place: the more interesting fact is that Stapledon was still flexible enough to follow this abstruse volume with one of his most imaginative and successful works, *The Flames*.

The Flames (1947)

The germ of the idea that was to evolve into *The Flames* can be found in *Last and First Men,* where the narrator claims to have found "evidence that in a few of the younger stars there is life, and even intelligence." In *Star Maker,* that compendium of strange forms of life, Stapledon returns to the idea of intelligent solar life and elaborates on it:

In the outer layers of young stars life nearly always appears not only in the normal manner but also in the form of parasites, minute independent organisms of fire, often no bigger than a cloud in the terrestrial air, but sometimes as large as the Earth itself. These 'salamanders' either feed upon the welling energies of the star in the same manner as the star's own organic tissues feed, or simply prey upon those tissues themselves. (*Star Maker,* p. 202)

The stars come to regard the salamanders as pests; and because each star is ashamed to admit to the others that it suffers from the salamandrian disease, each believes it is "the only sufferer and the only sinner in the galaxy." Since for the purposes of this novel the stars' minds are more important than those of their parasites, the narrator does not follow the salamanders much further. When it resurfaces in *The Flames,* however, the idea of salamandrian creatures of fire is treated with all the thoroughness and brilliance at Stapledon's command.

The Flames consists primarily of a long letter from a character nicknamed "Cass" because of his Cassandra-like prophecies, to a skeptical friend known as "Thos" (for "doubting Thomas"). The letter, written from an insane asylum, describes Cass's discovery that there are small flamelike creatures who live in fire and become dormant when the fire cools down. Originally they lived in the sun, but some were trapped in the massive balls of fire out of which the Earth and other planets were made. As the Earth cooled the living flames suffered more and more; now they lead sporadic existences, coming alive when a fire flares up and returning to a suspended state in rocks or other matter when the fire goes out. Potentially immortal, they can still be killed by a sudden change of temperature when a fire is doused with water.

The flames establish telepathic communications with Cass, and eventually, through one particular flame, they tell him why: they want the human race to set aside a large area where intense heat can be produced through a controlled nuclear reaction so that the flames can recover the lucidity that they knew while they were in the sun and can reach the remaining solar community through telepathy. Their purpose, they tell Cass, is to work toward the advancement of the spirit— a goal that Cass supports until he learns that in subtle ways the flames have been influencing him. Then he comes to see them as demonic forces whose goal is the enslavement of the human race, and after killing the flame that has been talking to him he begins a campaign of trying simultaneously to kill as many more flames as possible and to warn the public of the danger that the flames will attempt to take over the world. His campaign lands him in the asylum, where he writes his letter.

That Cass is committed to a mental hospital is both appropriate and ironic: appropriate because Cass is indeed insane, ironic because he is judged mad for all the wrong reasons. Cass's real madness lies not in believing that the flames exist (although since we see the action of the story through the skeptical eyes of Thos we can never be absolutely certain about the flames' existence) but in failing to see that they can lead the way to a more spiritually awakened world. An agnostic before all this happens, Cass turns into a religious fanatic determined to lead a crusade against the flames because he himself is too spiritually indolent to realize that his individual will is less important than the awakening of the entire world. What the flames propose is a symbiotic relationship between men and flames much like the relationship of Arachnoids and Ichthyoids in *Star Maker*: "We have a vision," says the flame, "of this planet as a true symbiotic organism, supported equally by your kind and my kind, united in mutual need and mutual cherishing" (58). Like the Arachnoids, man will contribute practical and manipulative skills; like the Ichthyoids, the flames will provide imagination, telepathic power, and spiritual insight. Together, the two kinds of beings will reach spiritual heights inaccessible to either species unaided by the other.

On its simplest level, *The Flames* may be read as one of Stapledon's many allegories of man's divided nature: the pleadings of the flames represent man's psychic or instinctive response to the spirit, our feeling that, as the flame puts it, "the goal of all action is the awakening of the spirit in every individual and in the cosmos as a whole" (35–36); but this feeling is warped and opposed by the subhuman element in us that prizes individuality above all else. Yet the story is so subtly ironic that any simple and straightforward reading is bound to be somewhat misleading. On the one hand, for example, the flames are figures of pure spirit and therefore of love. At the beginning of the novel the narrator is led (under the psychic influence of the flames) through a blizzard until he finds a rock that contains the flame that is to communicate with him; he takes the rock inside his cabin, puts it in the fire, and watches as the living flame emerges from the rock. Outside, the cold seems symbolic: "A queer terror seized me. . . . Something like this, I told myself, will really happen on the last man's last day, when the sun is dying, and the whole planet is arctic" (14). Clearly, the cold outside represents the indifference of a physical universe whose law of entropy will eventually doom all life; in taking the rock inside and allowing the flame to emerge, Cass takes the first step toward asserting the value of the spirit against the titans of darkness. The contrast between the warmth inside the cabin and the cold outside is reasserted later when Cass looks out of his window: "Outside, the cold ruled. The bare twigs of a climbing rose beside the window sparkled with frost in the lamp-light. The full moon was no goddess but a frozen world. The pale stars were little sparks lost in the cold void. Everything was pointless, crazy" (25).

In Cass's unbalanced state, however, the meaning of his experience is presented to him in an inverted form. The "icy and malignant presence" that he senses he takes to be the flames themselves, not the forces of darkness which they are committed to battling. Yet at all times Cass is aware of a conflict of wills within him, a conflict "between my sense of the excellence, the integrity and truthfulness of the flame and my new realization of the appalling danger that proud man should be spiritually enslaved to this formidable race" (64). The old revolutionary of *Old Man in New World* is intellectually incapable of accepting the message of the Fool even though on a deeper level he realizes its rightness; Cass, on the other hand, finds himself intellectually persuaded by the arguments of the flames but rebels because emotionally he is too immature to accept the fact that beings of another order can exert a psychic influence on him. How, he asks, can he be certain that his inclination to side with the flames is not simply the result of a quasi-hypnotic influence exercised on him by alien forces? We may well ask the same question—unless we recall that in *Last Men in London* Paul responded in similar fashion to the telepathic influence of the narrator on his mind until he came to see that the "Neptunian" half of his mind was his true self, the aspect of his personality that had escaped the prison of man's self-centered view of the universe and had adopted a more disinterested, more cosmic, perspective.

Eventually, Cass's attitude changes just as Paul's did. Some months after receiving the letter, Thos comes to visit Cass in the asylum and finds that he is still battling the flames—but for a different reason. The flames brought him to see their point of view, he says, and he found that a great deal had been happening. Various communities of flames in particularly stimulating environments had been able to reestablish telepathic contact with the flames on the sun, and they learned that the solar flames had in turn become part of a cosmic mind that was formed millions of years earlier. The cosmic mind had embarked on a great project: searching for, and consummating its union with, "the hypercosmical Lover," God (82). What the cosmic mind learned instead, though, was essentially what the forwards learned in *Darkness and the Light*: "Reality, it seemed, was wholly alien to the spirit, and wholly indifferent to the most sacred values of the awakened minds of the cosmos. It was indeed the Wholly Other, and wholly unintelligible" (83). The result has been a great splintering: the cosmic mind has ceased to exist, and throughout the universe there is conflict between one party which continues to hope for communion with God and another which insists on abandoning the struggle of the spirit in favor of a "purely epicurean" way of life (85). In the sun, however, there emerges a third party that combines the spiritual commitment of the first party and the agnosticism of the second. Cass pledges his loyalty to this new party but the terrestrial flames do not: they adopt the theistic view of the first party, and they persecute Cass in an attempt to convert him to their viewpoint. (Thus they finally become the malignant force that Cass once thought they were.) He tells Thos that the flames will try to kill him if he resists, and a few months later Thos learns that his friend has been burned to death in a fire whose cause cannot be determined. Incredulous to the end, Thos cannot bring himself to believe in the flames but publishes the whole account because of its psychological interest.

Thos may doubt, and the world may consider Cass mad, but Cass's final view is identical with Stapledon's. As Cass puts it, "Intellectual integrity, my dear man, is all very well; and it does compel us to be entirely agnostic about the constitution of the universe. But emotional integrity is just as important; and it compels me to be true to my perception of the spirit" (86). Ironically, the more spiritually awakened flames have been shattered by the experience of the cosmic mind into a sort of madness, while Cass, who is confined to a home for the insane, awakens into a truer perception of the role of spirit in the universe. The reversal of perspectives here recalls the second half of Edwin A. Abbott's Victorian fantasy, *Flatland*, a mathematical satire about a two-dimensional world.[8] After visiting a land of only one dimension, the narrator, a Square, is visited by a Sphere who takes him to Spaceland and thereby shows him the existence of the third dimension; but when the Square wants to know about the fourth and fifth dimensions, the Sphere denies that there can be more than three dimensions. Returning to Flatland, the two-dimensional Prometheus is imprisoned for preaching "The Gospel of Three Dimensions." Both in *The Flames* and in *Flatland*, the narrators first lag behind and then race ahead of the understanding of their mentors—and in each case, the saner and more lucid the vision of the narrator becomes, the more certain he is to be judged a lunatic or heretic.

The whole story may also be read in political and social terms. One of the primary differences between men and flames is that the flames are basically composite beings, almost like the Martians of *Last and First Men* or the avian and insectoid beings of *Star Maker*. The flame explains to Cass that "In some ways the whole flame race is almost like a single organism, unified telepathically. The individual is far less self-sufficient than with you. For all his higher psychical functions he depends on contact with his fellows, and so he needs a far less complex nervous system than you need" (30). The symbiotic world that the flames initially envision is in a sense a fully developed example of personality-in-community, with the flames representing the communal aspects of society and man representing the more individualistic and idiosyncratic element. In political terms, the flames are communistic, and Cass's rejection of their message is typical of the suspicious attitude of capitalistic countries toward communism. Following the conversion of Cass to the cause of the flames and Cass's new break with the flames over their theistic beliefs, the flames persecute Cass for failing to adopt the party line; here we see the dangers of conformity and intolerance that can await a communistic state that fails to awaken into a clear perception of the spirit. Stapledon may even be criticizing the Soviet Union for its development of a "state religion" of communistic dogma, although it is clear that he is generally very sympathetic toward the Russian state—and toward the flames.

As an example of controlled and sustained irony, *The Flames* is without parallel among Stapledon's works. The names of Cass and Thos are themselves ironic: Cassandra's gift of prophecy was a curse because her predictions were never believed, and Thos plays the role of doubting Thomas perfectly by refusing to believe what he cannot see—but what the reader is convinced must be true. Stapledon also plays ironically on the creative and destructive aspects of fire: we learn that the present advance in the spiritual powers of the flames was caused by the great conflagrations produced by World War II, or in other words by man's divisiveness and hatred, and later we see the flames themselves as destructive when they apparently murder Cass. Although it lacks the scope of several of Stapledon's other works, *The Flames* is a particularly subtle novel, one that rewards careful readers with an increased appreciation of the beauties and dangers of the life of the awakening spirit. If Stapledon's "observations of human beings as seen through the eyes of the flame creatures fail to reveal any new patterns of thought," as Sam Moskowitz believed when the book first came out,[9] then at least Stapledon's old observations are presented here with unusual precision and economy, and with the refined irony of the man who has come, like Cass, to see that there may be a thin line between madness and the clear perception of the spirit.

Chapter Six
Final Visions
A Man Divided (1950)

The related concepts of the "double" and man's divided personality have become important themes in literature of the past two hundred years as writers have developed a variety of means to demonstrate the complexities of human psychology. The double, a figure familiar to readers of Dostoevsky and Conrad, has become a standard fixture in modern narrative: thus in *Frankenstein*, as Harold Bloom has noted, "the monster and his creator are the antithetical halves of a single being,"[1] while in that decidedly non-Gothic novel *Mrs. Dalloway*, Virginia Woolf uses Clarissa Dalloway and Septimus Smith as symbolic doubles for each other. The concept of the fragmented personality, on the other hand, is a significant element in such works as the major prophecies of William Blake, Joyce's *Finnegans Wake*, and Hesse's *Steppenwolf*. More recently the true cases of "Eve White," "Sybil," and their other personalities have called attention to the rare, but uniquely interesting, psychological disorder known as "multiple personality," a condition that demonstrates in extreme form the fragmentation of personality or consciousness that may afflict all people to some extent.[2]

For many readers, the most famous case of multiple personality is undoubtedly the one originally described in Robert Louis Stevenson's thriller *The Strange Case of Dr. Jekyll and Mr. Hyde* (1886) and dramatized often in cinematic or televised adaptations. Stevenson's novel, which appeared in the year of Olaf Stapledon's birth, concerns a scientist whose experiments result in the emergence of a lower or demonic personality; in contrast, *A Man Divided*, published in the year of Stapledon's death, reverses the Jekyll and Hyde pattern by describing the dissociation of Victor Cadogan-Smith's mentality into the original "normal" personality and a higher, more spiritually awakened personality. Thus while Stevenson's allegory implies that man's fundamental baseness may erupt into plain view at any moment and may dominate his actions, Stapledon instead emphasizes the existence in each person of the will to light. Victor himself notes that all people contain the qualities that are isolated and polarized in his separate selves, and that his dilemma is a capsule version of "the whole social problem" of modern man (120).[3]

Victor's father, Sir Geoffrey Cadogan-Smith, was originally named Geoffrey Smith, but when he married a woman of higher social rank he hyphenated their names as a sign of his improved social status. The Cadogan-Smith name, later dropped by the awakened Victor in favor of plain "Smith," generally signifies the snobbishness that Victor has inherited from his father ("Cadogan" may suggest his frequently caddish behavior); as the book progresses, however, it becomes clear that the hyphenated name also represents the dual consciousness or split personality of its owner. As Cadogan-Smith, Victor is a self-centered conformist concerned largely with his advancement in business and society. As the awakened Victor, though, he is able to see beyond his own selfish concerns, into the lives and characters of others and on to the ineffable life of the spirit. After a number of brief awakenings at college, Victor awakens at an embarrassing moment and announces in the midst of his wedding that he and his fiancée are all wrong for each other. Instead, he falls in love with a waitress, Maggie, whose true beauty eludes all but the most sensitive. He continues in his awakened state for two years before reverting to his earlier personality. Then, the Dolt (as Victor calls him) regains consciousness and finds he cannot remember anything that has happened since the beginning of his abortive wedding ceremony. Soon the Dolt learns of the existence of his other self and despises the "true" Victor, but the situation suddenly changes again when the Victor Smith personality reappears. For ten years Victor remains in the awakened state, and feels secure enough to live with Maggie and raise a family. When the Dolt emerges again, he begins to develop a grudging admiration for his higher self; he even tries to take over the adult education classes that Victor has been teaching, although he proves incapable of rendering Victor's ideas very accurately, and eventually he overcomes his disgust at Maggie's appearance and begins to see why the real Victor was so attracted to her. For the last fifteen years of their life, Victor and the Dolt appear alternately, but Victor's appearances become less and less frequent. Their death comes when the Dolt, or rather a half-wakened form of the Dolt who has been enabled to see the problems of man's existence but cannot muster the faith that sustains the true Victor, commits suicide.

The theme of *A Man Divided* is a familiar one: earlier examples of divided personalities in Stapledon's fiction include the Flying Men in *Last and First Men*, who achieve a state of ecstatic awareness while they are in the air but lapse into a doltish condition on the ground; the Plant Men in *Star Maker*, who are doomed by their failure to strike a balance between their plant and animal natures; and Sirius, who is torn by the conflict between his "wolf nature" and his "human" potential. In *Darkness and the Light*, of course, the theme is developed on a worldwide scale; in *Last Men in London*, on the other hand, the influence of the Neptunian narrator produces in Paul a dual consciousness that in several respects is strikingly like Victor's. The real source of the theme, however, seems to lie in Stapledon's analysis of his own character. As he puts it in *Youth and Tomorrow*,

For my part, when I seem to myself to be most "awake," I do seem to see life from a new angle. I do precariously rise to a point of view less earth-bound than that of my ordinary experience. When I am most sensitively and most comprehensively aware of the universe (so far as it is within my ken) and of myself in it, and of those dear to me, I do find myself forced bewilderingly beyond the human view-point. . . . The evil and horror and cruel tragedy of existence floods in crushingly upon my ordinary little life; but at the same time something in me wakes, and accepts, not merely with resignation, but with trembling joy.[4]

Indeed, *A Man Divided* appears to be one of the most autobiographical of Stapledon's novels; only the description of Paul, in *Last Men in London*, the interludes in *Death into Life*, and *The Opening of the Eyes* are so clearly based on the author's own experiences. Yet a careful examination of the autobiographical elements in the novel indicates a need to qualify Sam Moskowitz's confident assertion that "*A Man Divided* transparently presents the events and agonizing intellectual conflicts by which Stapledon fashioned his philosophy, and gives an intimate picture of his personality and life from 1912 to 1948.''[5] Certainly some details of Victor's life reproduce elements of Stapledon's: they both attended Oxford, worked for a shipping firm, taught extramural classes, and participated in the educational programs of the British Army during World War II. Once these genuine correspondences are admitted, however, the lives of author and character begin to diverge. Unlike Stapledon, Victor spent no time in Egypt, served in the regular army rather than in a Quaker ambulance unit during World War I, joined the Communist party (although he later resigned his membership), and had three children to Stapledon's two. In addition, Sir Geoffrey Cadogan-Smith bears little real resemblance to Stapledon's beloved father, and for that matter it is unlikely that Olaf Stapledon was ever an unsufferable snob like the doltish Victor, even though he may have seemed so to himself later, as he indicates throughout *Youth and Tomorrow*.

Superficially, then, Victor seems only partly an autobiographical sketch. In the same way, the life of Maggie is very unlike Agnes Stapledon's: Maggie and Victor are not relatives, as Stapledon and his wife were (indeed they are not even from the same social class), and Maggie's birth in the Shetland Islands places her as far as possible from Agnes Stapledon's original home in Australia. Moreover, the narrator of *A Man Divided*—Harry Tomlinson, a college friend of Victor—insists that Maggie is physically very unattractive, while old photographs of Agnes Miller Stapledon reveal a rather handsome young woman. Yet Stapledon dedicated the novel to his wife, and Mrs. Stapledon quite rightly notes that the character of Maggie is in some ways based on her.[6] Maggie lacks the intellectual brilliance of her husband in his awakened state, but like Odd John's mother Pax, another character modeled on Agnes Stapledon,[7] she is a sensitive and clear-sighted woman whose compassionate love proves indispensable to a less stable personality.

In much the same way, although the details of Victor's life often fail to correspond precisely to those of Stapledon's career, the awakened Victor is certainly the *raisonneur* of the novel. In that role, he enunciates with unusual clarity Stapledon's view of man and of the struggle for spirit. The development of the doltish Victor into a half-wakened state, on the other hand, is important because his misinterpretations of the ideas of his more awakened self illustrate Stapledon's concern that his own ideas might not be fully understood. The narrator cites an appropriate example:

In his manuscript the true Victor had devoted much space to a careful study of the distinctively human personal relationship of fellowship or community. He had described it realistically in terms of self-awareness and other-awareness and the creation of a psychical "symbiosis," in which each individual becomes necessary to and is moulded by the other. The Dolt, I gather, had interpreted this to mean that a common spirit or soul emerged, with a life of its own over and above the life of the individual. The true Victor was infuriated by this "sentimental and romantic notion." (143)

The idea that there is no transcendent spirit apart from the spirits of individual beings is announced in several of Stapledon's books, beginning with *Last and First Men* where the narrator says that "Apart from this 'waking of individuals together' . . . the group-mind [of the Last Men] has no existence; for its being is solely the being of the individuals comprehended together." A similar, although broader, proclamation appears near the end of *A Man Divided* in a letter written by the true Victor shortly before his death: after telling his friend Harry that "Our fate depends at least in part on ourselves; or rather . . . on the strength of the universal spirit in us," he adds that "I don't mean by 'universal spirit', a universal 'being' or soul or person; I still mean just the ideal of spiritual living that beckons all half-awakened beings and claims possession of them" (182–83). There *may* be a God or universal spirit apart from man, as Victor admits; but he maintains Stapledon's consistently agnostic position that we should "be true to our own little insect intelligence, and not pretend we understand what is beyond our understanding." Those who claim that in his later years Stapledon came to believe in God should consider more carefully the clear evidence of *A Man Divided* that the general outlines of Stapledon's thought remained unchanged from his first novel to his last.

Nevertheless, certain aspects of Stapledon's philosophy seem to have been modified during the course of the years. His view of communism, for example, underwent subtle shifts of emphasis that make Victor seem considerably less sympathetic to communist thought and practice than one would expect from the earlier books. Never a doctrinaire communist, Stapledon was largely attracted to the economic theory of Marxism and the apparent dedication of the Russian people to the building of a new world-order. The major defect in communist practice noted in the early works is the single-mindedly materialistic view of man, a view that Stapledon regarded as a contradiction of the emotional and idealistic stimulus behind the Russian revolution. Such a materialistic denial of the spirit leads, in turn, to the blotting out of individuality within the communist state. What communism offers, on the other hand, is the termination of economic and social inequality and an all-important emphasis on community. Even when reacting against the practices of the communist state, Stapledon always assumes that his utopian world will be communistic in some way: a particularly appropriate example is the Pacific colony in *Odd John*, which is run along communist lines despite the emphasis on individuality which causes the Soviet Union to join forces with the other world powers that seek to destroy the colony.

In *A Man Divided*, again, Victor is set into opposition to the Communist party by the demand that he write articles falsely claiming "that the organization of the unemployed was entirely spontaneous, and not inspired by the Communists in the first place" (123). The communist doctrine that nothing is immoral if it is done in support of the revolution leads Victor to see the party as a perverter of the enlightened spirit. Moskowitz regards this whole section of *A Man Divided* as evidence that Stapledon was turned against communism by the 1949 Cultural and Scientific Conference for Peace in New York,[8] but in fact Stapledon's dissatisfaction with communism had been building for a long time; over a decade earlier, for example, his daughter had entered Oxford and had belonged to the Communist party for several weeks before discovering that she was being used by the party. Thus in *Beyond the "Isms,"* a book written during World War II while Russia was an ally of Britain, Stapledon felt compelled to protest against the "inadequate moral theory accepted by Communists" and to voice his suspicion that Russia's "superb achievement ... in respect of social creative planning" has become "warped by the kind of tyranny which is so apt to occur when there is more consciousness of political expediency than of the spirit."[9] Had

Stapledon lived to read Alexander Solzhenitsyn's *Gulag Archipelago*
he would have found ample evidence that the communist leaders of
the Soviet Union could prove at least as tyrannical as the Tsarist
regime that they replaced.

Perhaps more striking than the change in Stapledon's view of
communism is the modification of his brand of pacifism. While he
had never been an absolute pacifist, Stapledon's opposition to war was
so fundamental that until World War II he found it nearly impossible
to imagine circumstances that would justify armed conflict. The
contrast between his attitudes before and after the war can be most
sharply outlined through a comparison of the section on pacifism in
Waking World (1934)[10] and Victor's comments on pacifism in *A
Man Divided*. In the earlier book Stapledon had admitted that "to
fight for the new order *might* under certain circumstances become
necessary," but since "violence nearly always does more harm than
good" he proposes that those who want to build a higher world order
should refuse to support any national war. If their countries are
invaded, they should engage in "pacific 'non-co-operation' " with the
invaders:

Many of those who refused to carry out the instructions of the invaders
would, of course, be shot. There would be much brutality on the part of the
exasperated 'conquerors'. But you cannot in cold blood shoot a whole people.
If the people was resolute, and enough individuals were ready to accept
martyrdom, the foreign occupation would collapse.

With World War II, the death camps, and the destruction of whole
towns like Lidice and Oradour-sur-Glane in the background, it was no
longer possible for Stapledon to believe that "you cannot in cold
blood shoot a whole people." The struggle to reconcile his pacifistic beliefs
with the harsh reality of Nazi conquest and genocide is portrayed in
the pages of *A Man Divided*, where the more enlightened half of
Victor becomes a pacifist in the years between the world wars. When
World War II breaks out the "doltish" Victor, "believing himself to
be acting according to the best lights of his more gifted 'brother,' "
announces that he too is a pacifist (159). The true Victor, however,
has changed his mind by this time and has been "forced to the

conclusion that *this* war had indeed to be fought." Bringing his
influence to bear upon his other half, the higher Victor convinces the
lower that the war is necessary, whereupon the Dolt abandons pacifism
and tries to join the army, only to be rejected for psychological reasons.
His joy in being able to support the war demonstrates that the Dolt's
pacifism never ran very deep anyway, and that he has never fully
understood the principle of the advancement of the spirit—a principle
of which pacifism is only a small part.

His suicide provides further evidence that the Dolt, even in his most
advanced stages, has only a distorted view of the spiritual issues
confronting him. The Dolt's spiritual weakness is demonstrated during
a walk with Harry, when he decides to turn back because of a blizzard,
admitting that "the whole scene is too poignantly symbolical of the
universe. The desolation of these sweeping moors, the savage sleet, the
labour of every step, the early darkness, the whole physical world's
complete indifference to man, the way man himself has messed up
everything. . . . The fact is, life is getting me down. . . . Everything is
so bleak and hopeless, everything" (170). This passage, reminiscent of
the use of snow to represent the cold indifference of the universe in
The Flames, shows how inadequate is the Dolt's perception of the
importance of spirit within the universe: if he cannot see that the
universe sanctions the development of spiritual values, he can see only
futility and absurdity in human life.

Victor's suicide is the result of this distorted, incomplete vision. The
more awakened Victor, who wants to live, voices Stapledon's firm
belief that even a hopeless struggle for the spirit is worthwhile; as he
says, "the light of the Whole" transforms and redeems even the
darkest aspects of our existence (181). In this way, the "death-wish"
of the Dolt is properly seen as an aspect of the will to darkness and as
the failure of an individual will to accept something far beyond its
own understanding. Unlike the suicide of the Flying Men, and unlike
the suicide of John's colony, Victor's death signifies the triumph of the
dark will over man's higher self. Yet in devoting the last several pages
of the novel to a letter from the higher Victor to Harry, Stapledon
reiterates his faith that within the vast pattern of the universe
everything is meaningful:

... nothing is merely lost. Everything contributes. All the agonies, and the joys too, are gathered up into the whole single music of existence, the music which enjoys itself. And so the agony, which in the loneliness of our finite individuality is unredeemed and hideous and meaningless, contributes to the music, is significant; and in consciousness of its own significance in the whole it is itself transfigured into joy. (185)

Its status as the last novel completed by Olaf Stapledon and published before his death would give *A Man Divided* special significance in any case, but the book also has a certain importance in its own right. Although it is probably Stapledon's most conventional novel, the autobiographical basis of the novel and its depiction of the alternating personalities of the protagonist as representatives of the competing wills to darkness and light insure that the novel will provide its readers with an unusually clear assessment of the spiritual dilemma of modern man. The attitudes expressed in the book are important too, for they demonstrate Stapledon's ability to modify particular beliefs or views in accordance with circumstances without altering his philosophical "system" in any substantial way. The remarkable consistency of Stapledon's philosophical attitudes can be seen quite easily through a comparison of the end of *Last and First Men* and the end of *A Man Divided:* both are eloquent statements of the "agnostic mysticism" that looks past the darkness toward a light that may be only a creature of our own imagination, but is nonetheless worth striving for.

The Opening of the Eyes (1954)

When he died in September 1950, Olaf Stapledon left behind him several unpublished book manuscripts and three unpublished short stories. One of the longer works, *The Opening of the Eyes*, was later edited by Agnes Stapledon "from a very fine and rather complicated pencil copy" (ix)[11] and published in 1954 with a preface by the noted classical and biblical scholar E. V. Rieu, who describes Stapledon as "the most disturbing friend of mine whom I have ever had the hardihood to disagree with" (vii). Rieu had known Stapledon since their days at Balliol College and had for some time been Stapledon's editor at Methuen; in the prefaces of several of his books Stapledon gives Rieu credit for having made valuable suggestions, although how much Rieu really helped cannot be determined.

In any case, the selection of Rieu to write an introduction was natural enough, but Rieu's devout Christian beliefs seem to have led him to see his friend's attitude as more orthodox than it really was. He describes a meeting in London in 1949:

... Stapledon spoke with a confidence and a sense of achievement I had not previously observed in him. And very soon he told me all. He had reached the goal of his thinking; he had come to terms with reality; and comprehension had been added to acceptance. There was a note of serenity in his bearing which it is a pleasure to remember, now that he is gone. (viii–ix)

Unfortunately it is difficult to detect this "note of serenity" in the book itself. Writing a decade after Rieu, Sam Moskowitz also found that Stapledon "had accepted God" and "died with his lifelong mental anguish resolved,"[12] but in 1978 Moskowitz quoted a letter from Agnes Stapledon that termed Rieu's statement "much too simple and too final" and questioned Moskowitz's own contention that Stapledon abandoned communism and socialism at the end of his life.[13] In fact, a reading of *The Opening of the Eyes*, far from revealing its author's serenity or his acceptance of what we call God, shows that at the end of his life Olaf Stapledon was enuciating his major themes with the same degree of understanding and perplexity that can be found in the earlier works.

That is not to say that *The Opening of the Eyes* is typical of Stapledon's productions, for the book is actually the most abstract, mystical, and introverted of Stapledon's prose works. Divided into fifty-four brief chapters, the book takes the form of an extended meditation or apostrophe to Stapledon's "daimon," the dark-bright spirit whose purposes Stapledon probes in several of his books. Thus the work is more a confession than a novel, and the speaker here seems to be Stapledon himself rather than a fictionalized persona. There is a second voice, too, for the spirit seems at times to reply, often in order to chastise Stapledon for his incomplete understanding; but since Stapledon can never know for certain that this voice is not simply a projection of his own desire for the spirit, the speeches of the second voice are always somewhat ambiguous.

The book is so thoroughly paradoxical that it is almost impossible
to summarize its ideas without falsifying them in some way. Stapledon
begins by proclaiming "At last, at last I have seen you. My mind's
star, my heart's heart!"; but soon he admits that he does not know
exactly what he has seen. Again and again he states a proposition,
finds fault with it, then reasserts it in a new and more enigmatic way.
For example, in response to his belief that the dark and the bright, or
evil and good, are both necessary features of the spirit, the daimon's
reply voices an objection that many readers must have felt when they
saw the same ideas advanced in *Death into Life* and other novels:
"Were the masters of Buchenwald my ministers? Did I, for my
poetry's perfection, hunt down negroes for slaves, and pack them in
the slave-ships? Did I send children into the mines, congest the slums,
create the atom bomb? Is all the frustration and agony of all the
worlds in all the aeons mere imagery for my poetry?" (8). There is no
answer to this retort—no answer except that at times Stapledon
becomes "two selves, the one a tortured brute, the other exultant" (7).
The tortured, brutish mentality, like the doltish Victor, is incapable of
seeing that "the deeper the dark, the more radiant the light"; this he
can see only in his "exultant" phase, in which he attains the cosmic
perspective needed to resolve all aspects of existence into a meaningful
pattern. Whatever serenity or acceptance Stapledon found came only
in this more awakened state in which he saw glimpses of a higher
imaginative reality that cannot be rendered adequately in ordinary
human language. In part, the paradoxical form of *The Opening of the
Eyes*—and its failure as philosophical statement and literary art—
comes from this attempt to communicate the vision of the ineffable.

Parts of the book have a peculiar importance because of their
relation to other works or to Stapledon's political views. He refers to
the experience that inspired *Last and First Men* and the search for the
spirit throughout the subsequent novels:

Long ago (it was while I was scrambling on a rugged coast, where great
waves broke in blossom on the rocks) I had a sudden fantasy of man's whole
future, aeon upon aeon of strange vicissitudes and gallant endeavours in world
after world, seeking a glory never clearly conceived, often betrayed, but little
by little revealed. The seeing was you, and the glory was you. Since then,

year after year, I have tried to create in words symbols of that vision. The labour was you; and you were the splendour which those crude symbols failed to manifest. (29)

In a later chapter (49–52), he sits on a hill like the narrator at the beginning of *Star Maker* and speculates about other worlds, some of which may contain creatures like those encountered by the narrator of *Star Maker* on his cosmic journey of exploration. Perhaps even more important is Stapledon's review of "the whole ambiguous gospel of the comrades" (67–69), the section that formed the basis for Moskowitz's contention that Stapledon "renounced communism and socialism" in this book. In fact, what Stapledon states here is simply what he has said in one book after another: that a worldwide revolution is necessary, but that it must be a spiritual as well as a political revolution. Like the young pilot in *Old Man in New World*, and unlike the elderly hero of the revolution, Stapledon sees that any permanent political change must be founded on allegiance to the spirit: the communists, he says, "cannot see that without your commanding presence in the hearts and minds of leaders, the remaking will be false." He argues that "true revolutionaries" must be "saints" and that "If ever the leaders of the Revolution work with cruelty or lies, they harm the Revolution."[14] Each of these criticisms of dogmatic communism may be found in other works as well; the value of finding them here is that they demonstrate that the basic pattern of Stapledon's thought changed little during his twenty-year career as a writer.

It is difficult to find much else of enduring value in *The Opening of the Eyes*. Despite occasional stylistic brilliance, the prose is generally labored and stilted; the ideas of the book are laid out in a rather confusing manner; and there is no narrative line to hold the reader's attention and arouse intrest in the book as a philosophical statement. Rieu cites Mrs. Stapledon's opinion that the book is incomplete as well as unpolished, but the faults of the volume are so glaring that it is doubtful that it could have been worked into acceptable form without altering the basic concept of the book. Indeed, it seems likely that if Stapledon had lived longer he would have seen that *The Opening of the Eyes* was far below his standards and would have decided not to publish it, at least not in anything resembling its present form. Still, the publication of the book provides further evidence of the consistency of Stapledon's thought as he walked the "knife edge" of agnostic mysticism, and the imperfect construction of the book helps us to see how much more interesting Stapledon's ideas are when they are framed by an imaginative narrative.

4 *Encounters* (1976)

Composed sometime after World War II but not published until a quarter century after its author's death, *4 Encounters* is even less "finished" than *The Opening of the Eyes,* but in other respects it is a more successful piece of work. The narrative describes four apparently unrelated encounters with different sorts of people—a Christian, a scientist, a mystic, and a revolutionary—who expound their philosophies in dialogues with the narrator. Originally the plan was to include many more encounters—possibly fourteen[15]—but the four sequences that were written form a coherent group as varying points of view are balanced in a tightly controlled dialectic: the faith of the Christian is counterpointed against the skepticism of the scientist, the antimaterialistic bias of the mystic against the communist's rejection of the world of the spirit.

There are really five viewpoints argued in the novel, including the narrator's. Unlike the other characters, Stapledon—he is undoubtedly the narrator—is not convinced that he has found ultimate answers to the problems of existence. He sees, though, that each of the other characters has unintentionally oversimplified the nature of the universe and has grasped only part of the truth, like the Aesopian blind men whose descriptions of the elephant were limited by their contact with one part of the animal. The fundamentalist Christian, for instance, is sustained by his belief that he has been "saved" through faith in Christ, but in Stapledon's view the Christian's "present state of partial waking" makes him unable to "endure the severer vision" that transcends personal immortality (20).[16] The scientist, on the other hand, can see man only in material and biological terms that seem to point to the absurdity of man's existence; rejecting "spirit" and "goodness" as meaningless words, he argues that the search for pleasure should be man's purpose, and that science is useful largely because it makes us more comfortable. The universe, as he sees it, is devoid of meaning: "But beyond man, what is there? Just electro-magnetic radiation, and the fatal law of entropy" (43).

At the other extreme, the mystic does not believe in the reality of the material world. Convinced that only the spirit is real, he has withdrawn from human society, forsworn love, and dedicated himself to the life of contemplation. Stapledon argues for a more active, involved life, contending that "the life of the spirit is essentially the life of love, of concrete active love of individual persons" (56). He sees that in turning away from his fellow humans the mystic only reveals his lack of charity and his inability to realize that we must discover the world of spirit through the world of our senses. Stapledon's argument here is remarkably like that of William Blake, for whom any attempt to transcend the natural world in order to reach the realm of the imagination is bound to fail: as Blake puts it in *The Marriage of Heaven and Hell,* "Eternity is in love with the productions of time."[17] The converse of the mystic's error is illustrated by the young communist and his girl friend, who recognize the need for revolutionary political change but cannot see that political and social reform is a dead end unless it leads to a greater spiritual awareness. The narrator realizes that "these generous-hearted young people, through loyalty to the truth of Marx and Lenin, had blinded themselves to the deeper truth of Jesus, Buddha, Laotsze and all the saints" (94). As in *A Man Divided, The Opening of the Eyes,* and other works, Stapledon also criticizes the communists for operating as if the revolution is above all moral considerations: on the contrary, a revolution based on lies, murder, or torture will inevitably become despotic, and the measures used to bring about the revolution will insure the betrayal of all the ideals that inspired it.

While sitting at dinner with the revolutionaries, Stapledon says, "I bore witness to my certainty. I said my piece that you have heard so often, my piece about the spirit" (96). Like all of the book, these lines are addressed to his wife, but they might well be addressed to his faithful readers too, for they have also heard, many times, Stapledon's "piece about the spirit." Indeed, there is nothing new about the idea as it is presented here: the innovation of *4 Encounters* rests solely upon the narrative situations used to introduce Stapledon to each of the spokesmen for a "half-wakened" point of view. Everything about the book seems familiar, from the objections to the philosophies represented by the Christian and the others, to minor details like the reference to the murder of Lenin's brother (75).[18] Perhaps this is a clue to the major artistic dilemma facing Stapledon toward the end of his life when, like William Butler Yeats in "The Circus Animals' Desertion," he discovered that he could only "enumerate old themes."[19] There seems to have been no lessening of Stapledon's sense of mission in his later years—if anything, Stapledon probably was more committed than ever to the "awakening" of his small audience through his writings. But the primary appeal of his fiction had always been the ingenuity of his narratives, especially those that spanned unimaginable eons or described superhuman mentalities. Reduced to a series of debates, the argument loses its force. The real virtue of *4 Encounters* is that the work, incomplete though it may be, helps to clarify the distinction between Stapledon's point of view and the other ideas described in the book; but the reader who comes to *4 Encounters* after reading the more imaginative earlier volumes is unlikely to find that one virtue sufficient to sustain his interest in the book.

The Short Stories

The recent publication of Olaf Stapledon's short stories[20] has revealed a side of Stapledon's fiction that has long gone neglected. The reasons for that neglect are not hard to find: only five short stories by Stapledon are known to exist, and only two of the five made their way into print during their author's lifetime. Furthermore, given Stapledon's tendency to write extravagant fictions that often seem too wide-ranging to be called novels, it may be hard to imagine that he could stay within the far stricter limitations of the short story. Yet an examination of Stapledon's shorter fiction reveals, in miniature, the same originality of conception and skillful control of his materials that is found in many of the longer works.

Perhaps most interesting are "A World of Sound" and "The Man Who Became a Tree," two stories in which the author attempts to portray alternate modes of consciousness or other forms of reality. "A World of Sound," probably the earlier of the two, is a dream-vision in which the narrator falls asleep at a concert and imagines himself in a world populated not by solid creatures but by "sound-figures." Much like the narrator of *Star Maker,* he explores his new world, discovering that he has a musical body that he can move by readjusting its "shape" or tonal pattern. He also finds that he has a girl friend but she slips away from him. Later he encounters a sound-monster, which pursues him until at last he awakens from his nightmare to find that the concert has ended. The plot, however, is not particularly important here, for the story appears to be largely an exercise in pure imagination. Since *Star Maker* was published only a year after "A World of Sound" first appeared, the modestly successful attempt to describe a totally new sort of universe in the story may be seen as a harbinger of the more ambitious undertakings of Stapledon's cosmic masterpiece.

In execution if not in conception, "The Man Who Became a Tree" is an even finer story. Again, the title should be taken literally: a man falls asleep under a tree and finds his consciousness leaving his body in order to experience the life of the tree. At first the story appears to be a dream, but soon we find that, in the manner of Kafka's "The Metamorphosis," the whole story is to be regarded as actually happening. Unlike Gregor Samsa, however, Stapledon's character is not the victim of a malign and absurd universe; instead, he rejoices in the condition that opens him to a wide range of new experiences. He alternates between two modes of experience: the human or analytic mode, which seems to correspond to the medieval concept of the rational soul, and the "arboreal" or purely sensory mode, which parallels the vegetative *anima.* In a subtle reversal of the medieval pattern, however, the tree-man finds that enlightenment comes not through the suppression of the vegetative mode of consciousness but through a combination of the self-consciousness of the human being and the tree's awareness of its "fundamental physiological processes, its whole vegetative life." Season after season, the tree's awareness expands, eventually passing beyond the life of the individual tree to encompass "the common awareness of all trees, nay, all terrestrial vegetation." Since this pattern of gradually widening consciousness is familiar to readers of *Star Maker,* we are not surprised to find that it culminates in a mystic vision of God. The conclusion of the story shows that the man's life as a tree has led him to the dispassionate objectivity of the cosmic point of view: "When at last foresters came, and with saw and axe cut through the aging trunk, the man's mind was at least partially attuned to the deeper reality. The sharp pain, though painful, was yet acceptable."

In all probability, the earliest of Stapledon's stories was "East Is West." Like "A World of Sound," this story is a dream-vision, but the alternate world depicted in the story is largely a satiric commentary on our world rather than an attempt to conceive an alternate form of reality. The story takes place in 1934 and involves a simple reversal: Britain and other European countries are just beginning to assert themselves against the colonialist domination of Japan, which has ruled much of the world for centuries because of its early lead in "mechanical invention and commercial organization." In the alternate world, the narrator and his "wife," Betty, have Japanese house guests who want to stay out of sight because of popular sentiment against "the Yellows." In the climax of the story, they listen to a radio broadcast by the English queen, who is treated with all the absurd obeisance that the Japanese were showing toward their emperor in the real world of 1934. The queen urges her people to overthrow the Japanese, and announces that she has declared war on the oppressors. There is a great deal of imagination in the description of the Wirral peninsula after centuries of Japanese domination, and the satiric effects of the story are clear if occasionally heavy-handed, but the dream ends before Stapledon has had a chance to develop his ideas and his plot situation adequately.

The other stories are "A Modern Magician" and "Arms Out of Hand." The lesser of the two, "A Modern Magician" is a modest allegory of the destructive effects of *hubris* in a man whose inability to use his power maturely leads to his death. As such, it provides readers with a clearly individualized example of a problem that in *Last and First Men* plagues the First Men through their existence: the difficulties caused by the rapid development of technological power (or psychic power, in the story) at a time when man's moral or social sensibilities are still very immature. The narrative line is clear and simple, and while the story is a minor piece it is generally an effective one.

"Arms Out of Hand," however, is a more ambitious undertaking. As a story of a split personality, it adumbrates the theme of *A Man Divided,* but the uncharacteristically Gothic tone of the story helps to give it an identity of its own. That the story is to be read allegorically is indicated by the name of its protagonist, Sir James Power: as we discover, Sir James has abused his power over his employees, and in the course of the story he loses his power over his right hand, which begins to act independent of Sir James's conscious will. Hiding beneath his veneer of liberalism, Sir James is torn between the primitive urge to dominate others—expressed by his right hand—and the more awakened sense of others as separate persons, a sense that emerges through his left hand. (The connection with the right and left wings of the body politic is clear enough, but Stapledon is too subtle to press the issue.) Thus when Sir James attempts to write a letter defending several young men who have been arrested on phony charges of sedition, he finds that his right hand communicates an altogether different sentiment—that the "young swine" should be suppressed before it is too late. The right hand continues to get out of line, as Sir James's baser nature takes over, so finally he binds it to his body. With the right hand incapacitated, the higher personality emerges. For example, Sir James has always suppressed his interest in his secretary, Miss Smith. Now, when his right hand is in control, he grabs her around the waist in a libidinous outburst of purely sexual desire; but when the left hand is ascendant, he kisses her hand and sees her, if only momentarily, as a separate center of consciousness who must not be treated selfishly. The tug-of-war between his separate personalities proves too much for Sir James, however, and in the end he must be committed to a home for the mentally disturbed.

In none of the stories do we see a major idea that is not found throughout Stapledon's other writings, but even the least of the stories are further evidence of the power and originality of Stapledon's fertile imagination. Although we associate Stapledon with the breathtaking scope of *Last and First Men* or *Star Maker,* the stories demonstrate that he could also work effectively within the narrower confines of a story like "The Man Who Became a Tree" or "Arms Out of Hand." There is little chance that Stapledon's few stories will ever have a major impact on other science fiction writers; whatever influence Stapledon wields will come from his longer works. Still, it is interesting to note that as early as the 1930s, during the celebrated Golden Age of pulp science fiction, Olaf Stapledon could write an occasional short story with all the control and poise found in his novels and in the short stories of later writers.

Chapter Seven

The Heritage of Olaf Stapledon

Theme and Vision

In the half century since the publication of *Last and First Men*, Olaf Stapledon has occupied an honored but uneasy position within the field of science fiction. On the one hand he is frequently praised by critics, writers, and others familiar with his works, and he has been credited with introducing a wide range of themes that readers have come to associate with the genre. Basil Davenport, calling Stapledon "an inspiration to good writers and a veritable quarry for hacks," suggests that Stapledon was probably the first science fiction writer to deal with such important themes as the sympathetic and abhorrent qualities of a mutant, human intelligence in a dog, the devastation of Earth by nuclear power, the idea that the superman may be both the "potential savior and actual victim of mankind," strange nonhuman (and even nonanimal) intelligences, and genetic engineering.[1] Stapledon is often said to have originated other themes and motifs too: galactic empires, symbiotic relationships between beings of different races or species, and the possibility that the mind can travel through time and space independent of the body, for example, are all ideas that can be traced to *Star Maker*. On the other hand, the lack of straightforward narrative lines and the emphasis on philosophical ideas places Stapledon's fiction in a different category from works of the *Star Wars* variety and alienates many readers who are simply looking for entertainment. The result is that Stapledon is treated as an oddity: respected but not widely read, he is accepted as an important figure in the field so that science fiction fans can claim as their own at least one writer of undoubted seriousness, yet with several significant exceptions, his influence on the field has been confined to the introduction of imaginative plot devices.

If the current upsurge of critical interest in serious science fiction continues, however, we can expect renewed attention to the works of writers like Stapledon, not only by critics of science fiction but by students of "mainstream" literature as well. The line separating science fiction from "real literature" has become very thin in recent decades as important writers like Flann O'Brien, Anthony Burgess, and Doris Lessing have used techniques of science fiction in their novels. Lessing, in fact, has objected to the strange but prevalent habit of classifying science fiction simply as escapist literature: in the introduction to her first science fiction novel, *Shikasta*, she writes, "I do think there is something wrong with an attitude that puts a 'serious' novel on one shelf and, let's say, *First and Last Men* [*sic*] on another."[2] Despite the confusion about the title of Stapledon's novel, *Shikasta* may owe a great deal to *Last and First Men*; its emphasis on genetic and evolutionary themes, its sympathetic portrayal of extraterrestrial beings, and the style of its historical and sociological summations all suggest that Stapledon influenced Lessing's conception of her novel. A kinship with Stapledon may also be detected in the cosmic perspective of a passage like the following:

We are all creatures of the stars and their forces, they make us, we make them, we are part of a dance from which we by no means and not ever may consider ourselves separate. But when the Gods explode, or err, or dissolve into flying clouds of gas, or shrink, or expand, or whatever else their fates might demand, then the miniscule items of their substance may in their small ways express—not protest, which of course is inappropriate to their station of life—but an acknowledgement of the existence of irony: yes, they may sometimes allow themselves—always with respect—the mildest possible grimace of irony.[3]

The impact of Stapledon's themes and techniques is apparent in certain other writers, too. The time schemes reproduced in some of the novels and stories of Robert A. Heinlein's Future History Series, for instance, are simply more detailed examples of the type of time scale used in *Last and First Men* and in *Star Maker*. Like Stapledon's time scales, Heinlein's indicate the scope and coherence of his vision, although in later years Heinlein was to deviate from his own pattern. Stapledon's influence surfaces in more important ways in Clifford D. Simak's *City* (1952) and Theodore Sturgeon's *More Than Human* (1953). In Sturgeon's novel, several outcasts establish a symbiotic relationship reminiscent of the sexual groups of the Last Men or the Pacific colony in *Odd John*. Together, the members of the group become one superhuman individual, *Homo gestalt*, perhaps the most complexly conceived example of group mentality of the post-Stapledon era. In *City* there is another example of symbiosis, but over the millenia the partners in the relationship—men, dogs, and robots—go their own ways, and by the time the story is told, the dogs regard the existence of man as a fable. There is a striking originality in the construction of *City* as a series of stories from different epochs, each with a mock-critical introduction, but the possibility of developing the story of man's history over thousands of years was undoubtedly influenced, directly or indirectly, by the scope of *Last and First Men*. The antagonism between mankind and a race of superhuman mutants, the possibility that man could evolve in order to exist on another planet (Jupiter), the insistence on truly understanding the point of view of another being or race, the challenge to conventional morality—these and other elements of Simak's book indicate a profound debt to Stapledon.

The Reaction: C. S. Lewis

Ironically, the first science fiction writer whose work was significantly affected by Stapledon's was someone whose vision of the world was in most ways quite different from the ideas he encountered in *Last and First Men*. That was C. S. Lewis, the Cambridge don, literary critic, and author of children's fantasies, who saw in Stapledon a challenge to his own Anglican orthodoxy. About the genesis of *Out of the Silent Planet*, the first volume of his science fiction trilogy, Lewis wrote,

What immediately spurred me to write was Olaf Stapledon's *Last and First Men* and an essay in J. B. S. Haldane's *Possible Worlds*, both of which seemed to take the idea of such [space] travel seriously and to have the desperately immoral outlook which I try to pillory in Weston. I like the whole inter-planetary idea as a *mythology* and simply wished to conquer for my own (Christian) point of view what has always hitherto been used by the opposite side.[4]

For Lewis, the "opposite side" was "a sort of creed which might be called 'scientific humanism.' " Stapledon, he believed, was "tarred with the same brush" of this creed as people like Wells, Haldane, and George Bernard Shaw.[5] Lewis's attack on Stapledon was often strident, as it was when he declared that "*Star-Maker* [*sic*] ends in sheer devil worship."[6] At other times, he was ready to concede that the form of *Last and First Men,* although "not novelistic at all," was "the right form for the theme,"[7] and in the preface to *That Hideous Strength* he admitted that "I admire [Stapledon's] invention (though not his philosophy) so much that I should feel no shame to borrow."[8] Expressions of admiration for Stapledon's literary talent notwithstanding, Lewis made little use of Stapledonian techniques in his trilogy, whose form owes more to David Lindsay's 1920 fantasy, *A Voyage to Arcturus,* than to any other single novel. An examination of the trilogy is of interest here primarily because in his novels Lewis constructed a serious argument against ideas that he associated with Stapledon and others who are "tarred with the same brush" of scientific humanism.

The trilogy opens with *Out of the Silent Planet* (1938), in which Ransom, a character remarkably like Lewis, is kidnapped and taken to Mars. His abductors, Weston and Devine, have been to Mars before and have returned to Earth in search of a victim for the human sacrifice that they believe (erroneously) is desired by a Martian race; ultimately they hope to colonize Mars so that Weston can further his plan for expanding the human race throughout the solar system and so that Devine can get rich from Martian gold. On Mars, Ransom discovers that Malacandra (the real name for Mars) is inhabited by several races of intelligent creatures who live in harmony with each other and who obey the "eldils" (angels). Earth, we learn, is the "silent planet" because it was put under a sort of interplanetary interdiction after the Fall of Man. Returned safely to Earth by the eldils at the end of the first book, Ransom goes to Venus in the second volume, *Perelandra* (1943). There, he discovers an Eve-like woman faced with temptation by Weston—or, rather, Satan, who has taken over Weston's body. Through Ransom's efforts, Perelandra remains an unfallen world. The last book, *That Hideous Strength* (1945), shifts the battle of good and evil to Earth, where an organization ironically called N.I.C.E. (National Institute for Coordinated Experiments) tries to take over a college town in order to further its plan to indoctrinate mankind in its materialistic and antireligious precepts. Good triumphs over evil—and religion over scientific materialism—when Ransom and his friends resurrect Merlin, who helps them defeat N.I.C.E.

The attack on Stapledon and Haldane, whom Lewis almost invariably associated with one another even though their views on a variety of subjects were actually quite divergent, is most evident in the portrayal of Weston in the first two volumes of the trilogy. Men like Weston, Lewis says in *Perelandra*, spread their ideas through "obscure works of 'scientifiction' " and through "little Interplanetary Societies and Rocketry Clubs." Their purpose is to overcome "the vast astronomical distances which are God's quarantine regulations," so that eventually, "planet after planet, system after system, in the end galaxy after galaxy, can be forced to sustain, everywhere and for ever, the sort of life which is contained in the loins of our own species," even if that event entails the destruction of species from other planets.[9] In *Out of the Silent Planet*, the attack is handled more skillfully. Weston is summoned before Oyarsa, the chief eldil of Malacandra, but proves to be so thoroughly debased that he cannot even see Oyarsa, let alone speak his language with any assurance. Ransom undertakes the task of translating Weston's ideas for Oyarsa, and the result is an ironic alternation between the apparent dignity and logic of Weston's ideas when he first expresses them, and the full force of their wickedness when Ransom translates the message. Thus Weston's assertion that "Our right to supersede you is the right of the higher over the lower" becomes more obviously sinister when it is rephrased as "it would not be the act of a bent *hnau* [a wicked being] if our people killed all your people."[10]

In this sequence, Lewis was thinking primarily of the destruction of the Venerians in *Last and First Men*; apparently he misinterpreted Stapledon's treatment of the episode as indicating approval, or at best only mild disapproval, of racial murder. That this attitude is far different from Stapledon's is clear to virtually any reader, although Stapledon's refusal to condemn unequivocally the destruction of the Venerians provides Lewis with some ammunition for his attack. Actually, a more fundamental, and potentially more serious, misconstruction of Stapledon's beliefs is at the heart of Lewis's argument. If he had read *Star Maker* by the time he wrote *Out of the Silent Planet*, Lewis would have recognized that Stapledon agrees with him that intelligence, or spirit, may exist in many forms other than our own, and that some other species may be far more spiritually developed than mankind. In treating the desire to explore space merely as another, more dangerous, example of the kind of colonial exploitation that Europeans had practiced in various parts of the world, Lewis ironically reversed the perspective of Wells's *The War of the Worlds*, where the Martians are depicted as an invading colonial army. The problem is that Lewis is not content with his ironic point, but instead develops an argument against the morality of all space travel, and even against all writers who "take the idea of such travel seriously."

Lewis is certainly right about one thing: Stapledon's view of the place of man in the universe is based partly on modern science, although Stapledon frequently noted the inadequacy of a *purely* scientific view of reality. Lewis, on the other hand, is in revolt against the age of science and against the agnosticism of the modern world in general. If the traditional, orthodox Christian view of the human condition is correct, then man is simply a fallen creature who must spend his life trying to follow God's commands in order to gain entry into heaven. Such a view implies sharp limitations on human conduct, and perhaps even sharper limitations on human knowledge. As a Milton scholar, Lewis would have recalled Raphael's warning to Adam in *Paradise Lost*:

> Heav'n is for thee too high
> To know what passes there; be lowly wise:
> Think only what concerns thee and thy being;
> Dream not of other Worlds, what Creatures there
> Live, in what state, condition or degree,
> Contented that thus far hath been reveal'd
> Not of Earth only but of highest Heav'n.

(VIII, 172–78)

For Stapledon, however, the role of man in the universe is unlikely to be revealed, much less neatly defined, by supernatural messengers. He never doubted—although he could not prove—that there was something real above the material realm, something he called "spirit"; but he regarded the growth of spirit in individual persons not as a passport to eternal life but as the first step toward a larger racial awakening, one that would help man understand the purpose of his existence more fully than Olaf Stapledon, the half-wakened author of scientific fantasies, ever could.

Between Lewis and Stapledon there are obvious, and fundamental, differences. One was a political conservative, the other a socialist; one held orthodox Christian views while the other was an agnostic; one regarded the other's interest in space travel as evidence of his immorality. Despite occasional references to his respect for Stapledon's "invention," Lewis seems to have cherished these differences: once he had pegged Stapledon as a "scientific humanist" (a label Stapledon would have rejected), Lewis could read Stapledon's novels only as expressions of a philosophy that was altogether alien to his vision of man. He failed to see that despite their many differences, he and Stapledon had several ideas in common. As the "mad worlds" sequence of *Star Maker* indicates, Stapledon was quite aware that space travel could become such an obsession that it might lead to exploitation and conquest on the part of even a spiritually "awakened" species. Like Lewis, he opposed totalitarianism and other attempts to undermine the value of individual beings, and he was careful to remind his readers that there was real danger in regarding the group as an entity separate from, and superior to, the members of that group. Furthermore, as Scholes and Rabkin observe, "Stapledon was no human-racist either; he was as ready to accept the whole of creation and praise it as Lewis himself."[11] Lewis's works may be read as simple allegories of the struggle between good and evil; Stapledon, meanwhile, explicitly rejects some of the premises of Lewis's arguments. But their works also contain evidence of a deeper kinship: a desire to assert the enduring importance of human life—indeed, of all kinds of intelligent life—and an insistence that there can be no real spiritual advancement unless we recognize and accept the need of each individual being to be free to develop in his own way.

The Inheritors: Arthur C. Clarke and Stanislaw Lem

When Arthur C. Clarke's most famous novel, *Childhood's End,* was published in 1953, Lewis called the book "better than any of Stapledon's."[12] It's not entirely clear how Lewis meant that remark to be taken, but it seems likely that Stapledon came to mind because *Childhood's End* owes so much to Clarke's reading of Stapledon's works. In his introduction to *The Lion of Comarre & Against the Fall of Night,* Clarke wrote that Stapledon's "tremendous saga of future history, *Last and First Men,*" was the greatest influence on his own work:

I came across this volume in the public library of my birthplace, Minehead, soon after its first appearance in 1930. With its multimillion-year vistas, and its roll call of great but doomed civilizations, the book produced an overwhelming impact upon me. I can still remember patiently copying Stapledon's "Time Scales"—up to the last one, where "Planets Formed" and "End of Man" lie only a fraction of an inch on either side of the moment marked "Today."[13]

In the 1940s, Clarke and Stapledon knew each other through the British Interplanetary Society. When Stapledon presented his talk on interplanetary man at the October 1948 meeting of the Society, Clarke chaired the discussion and offered his own views of some points raised in the lecture. He contended, for example, that interstellar travel might not be as difficult as Stapledon imagined, but he argued that participation in a galactic culture was almost certainly beyond man's capacities.[14] While he disagreed with Stapledon about a variety of details, however, Clarke was sufficiently impressed by *Last and First Men* to have said that "The book transformed my life."[15] It is not surprising, then, that various themes developed in Stapledon's works are also found in Clarke's science fiction.

Clarke pointed to what may be the most important of those themes when he said, in *Profiles of the Future,* that "the whole galaxy, as Olaf Stapledon suggested long ago, may be evolving toward consciousness, if it has not already done so."[16] The best example of this theme in Clarke's own fiction is found in *Childhood's End.* Since that book makes use of many ideas derived from Stapledon's books, we need to examine it carefully.

Childhood's End opens with glimpses at two German scientists, one working for the Americans and the other for the Russians, as each tries to insure that his adoptive country reaches the moon before its rival. The race comes to an end when giant spaceships appear in the skies and alien beings known as the "Overlords" begin their benevolent rule over Earth. In the ensuing years national governments become insignificant as the Overlords, who rule from their spaceships without being seen, use the secretary-general of the United Nations as the agent of their administration. Fifty years later when they finally reveal themselves, human beings realize why the invaders have kept their appearance secret for so long: the Overlords have all the physical features associated with the Devil. Ironically, under their enlightened guidance, man enters a "golden age" of peace and prosperity. In time, however, there is a strange change that begins with a few children and soon spreads to all the children on Earth: they develop extraordinary mental powers and seem at times to be unaware of their physical surroundings. Eventually, the children actually become one great mental being, and after many years of testing its powers on Earth the being that was humanity joins the Overmind, the great mental being that is served by the Overlords. The end of the Earth is watched by the Overlords out in space and is reported by the "Last Man," Jan Rodricks, who perishes as Earth is consumed by the departure of the mental being.

The Overmind is of course Clarke's version of the cosmic spirit in *Star Maker* and *Death into Life*, but there is one major difference: while Stapledon insists that some sort of individual consciousness is retained even as the individual spirit is absorbed into the cosmic spirit, Clarke makes no such stipulation. Likewise, the evolution of the children into one being recalls the "racial experience" described in *Last and First Men* and *Last Men in London*, but while Stapledon describes a temporary union of individual minds, Clarke implies a total obliteration of individuality through union with others. The structure of the book is more clearly indebted to Stapledon in its depiction of the evolution toward pure consciousness, which here is treated as a series of stages toward the unification of man's divided spirit. At the beginning of the novel, the competition between America and Russia implies deep divisions among countries, while the use of German scientists by both sides suggests that the partition of Germany is the ultimate example of man's war against himself. The gradual unification of the human spirit appears first in political terms, with the abolition of national governments and the formation of a world state, just as in *Last and First Men* the World State can be seen as the result of man's struggle toward a spiritual awakening. Finally, man becomes not merely one political being, but one great mentality, thereby endorsing Stapledon's position that a utopian society can lay the groundwork for man's evolution into a higher form of life.

Childhood's End contains several other ideas that may be traced to Stapledon, including the use of a "Last Man" to report on man's end, the destruction of Earth through sheer mental power, and even the idea that invaders from outer space might well be more spiritually advanced than man. Clarke's reference to "the strange symbiosis between the Overmind and its servants"[17] strikes a note familiar to readers of *Star Maker,* and the curious visions of mental phenomena in Clarke's book may also have been suggested by certain passages in *Star Maker* that attempt to describe the indescribable. More obviously, Clarke makes use of a concept of time and racial memory that is similar to the one underlying the narration of *Last and First Men* and *Last Men in London,* an idea that Stapledon uses again in parts of *Odd John* and *Star Maker.* Both writers assume the possibility that the mind can transcend the limitations of time and establish contact with a mind from another era. Thus in *Childhood's End,* Jean Morrel unwittingly makes contact with the mind of her unborn (indeed unconceived) child during a seance. Later we realize that man's traditional image of the devil has nothing to do with an earlier visit by the Overlords, who have never been to Earth before the twentieth century: instead, man's collective unconscious "remembers" their future visit and associates their image with evil because they will preside over the end of the human race.

The heritage of Olaf Stapledon is reflected in other works by Clarke as well. Purely mental beings may be found in the Star-Child at the end of *2001: A Space Odyssey* (1968) and in the creature known as Vanamonde, who appears both in *Against the Fall of Night* (1953) and in the expanded version of the same book, published under the title *The City and the Stars* (1956). Peter Brigg has also noted that the idea of "planet-sized space vessels" in *Rendezvous with Rama* and other works by Clarke is an adaptation of an idea found in the ninth chapter of *Star Maker*.[18] Clarke's novels lack the didacticism of Stapledon's, and their plots and characterization owe more to the novels of Jules Verne and H. G. Wells than to Stapledon's more difficult fictional forms, but within the field of contemporary science fiction Clarke demonstrates more clearly than any other writer the influence of Stapledon's ideas, including the paradoxical affirmation of man's significance against the vastness and indifference of space.

Stapledon's influence may also be seen in some of the novels of Stanislaw Lem, the Polish writer who, like Clarke, has declared his admiration for Stapledon.[19] No less than Stapledon, Lem satirizes man's assurance that the universe has been created for man and may be adequately viewed in anthropomorphic terms. One consequence of the attack on anthropomorphism is that Lem creates species of intelligent life reminiscent of some of the strangest life forms encountered in the pages of Stapledon's books. In *The Invincible* (1964), in fact, there is a skillful reversal of the Martian invasion in *Last and First Men*: sent to a distant planet to discover why a previous expedition ended in failure, the explorers discover that their predecessors were killed by "clouds" of microscopic crystals remarkably like Stapledon's Martians. Likewise, the intelligent "ocean" of *Solaris* (1961) bears comparison with some of Stapledon's creations in *Star Maker*.

The plot of *Solaris* is deceptively simple. Kelvin, a scientist specializing in "Solaristics" (the study of the planet Solaris), arrives at the space station circling Solaris and finds the place in chaos. People—or, rather, alien beings who look like people and *think* that they are people—have been appearing to the members of the station. Soon, one appears to Kelvin, looking exactly like Rheya, his former lover who committed suicide because of him. It is decided that these "Phi-beings," as they come to be called, are created by the "ocean" from the minds of the men; but whether Solaris is deliberately creating these beings, and what reasons it might have for such action, remains unknown. Here, as in *The Invincible*, man's efforts to understand an alien form of intelligence prove futile since we can conceive of intelligence only when it comes clothed in the garment of the human form.

Stapledon, of course, makes much the same point time after time. Thus the Second Men and the Martians each fail to recognize that the other is a form of intelligent life, while the difficulties involved in dealing with an intelligent dog in *Sirius* prove almost insignificant compared to the problem of communicating with the flame-creatures of *The Flames*. Yet there is a difference: in Stapledon's works we can eventually establish contact with alien beings, perhaps even join in the formation of a "cosmic spirit" and thereby overcome the limitations of our purely human perspective. In Lem's novels, however, there appears to be no way out of the epistemological dilemma, no way of achieving the "cosmic" perspective advocated by Stapledon, because the human mind lacks the capacity to view the universe in any terms other than those suggested by our experience as human beings. Thus the science of Solaristics is at once a failure—necessarily so, since it is the study of something that, by definition, is beyond our comprehension—and an example of our misplaced faith in the unlimited possibilities of scientific investigation. As in the World State of *Last and First Men*, too, Lem's science has become a type of religion: there is even a book called *The Little Apocrypha,* which details discarded (i.e., heretical) theories about Solaris, while in another volume, *Introduction to Solaristics,* Kelvin reads that contact with Solaris has become the equivalent of divine revelation, and that the "cornerstone" of the creed of Solaristics is "the hope of Redemption."[20]

If Lem and Stapledon are superficially alike in many ways, the reason for the many similarities may be their rejection of what Stapledon called the "isms." Creeds, dogma, simplistic and reductive beliefs of all kinds, from Christianity to communism, from the cult of Gordelpus to Solaristics, may all have a function, but all are to some extent false—or, to put the matter in a more positive light, all neglect aspects of experience necessary for man's appreciation of higher spiritual values. If Lem's treatment of the human dilemma is more fundamentally ironic than Stapledon's, it is no less serious, and no less valuable. As a contribution to the growing list of science fiction books that have genuine literary merit, Lem's work ranks as a worthy successor to that of Olaf Stapledon.

Conclusion

Ezra Pound once distinguished between two types of writers who deserve our attention: the "inventors," those creators of new literary forms whose work represents a break with past styles or ideas, and the "masters," those who perfect a literary technique or develop its potential more fully than others have.[21] Within the field of science fiction, Stapledon might well be considered both an inventor and a master, and it is clear that his works are destined for inclusion among the classics of the genre. His reputation outside the field, however, is less secure. Once taken seriously as a major writer, one whose works deserved to be reviewed by the likes of Arnold Bennett, J. B. Priestley, and Bertrand Russell, one whose essays were routinely solicited for publication alongside those of other leaders of the British intelligentsia, Stapledon has more recently suffered from being labeled a writer of "science fiction." Another factor working against Stapledon is that while his books are certainly avant-garde, they do not contain the sort of literary experimentation most favored by the critical establishment. Compared to Joyce, Woolf, Faulkner, and others whose works are central to the received canon of modern literature, for example, Stapledon's novels contain few experiments with shifting points of view or with the direct rendition of consciousness through language. The style of his books seems Victorian: it is graceful, controlled, but at times perhaps a little inflexible, as evidenced by the fact that the style of *Star Maker* never changes even though its narrator undergoes the most extraordinary widening of consciousness imaginable. To some extent the refusal to follow the lead of someone like Joyce may simply represent Stapledon's recognition of his own limitations, but it is also the result of Stapledon's desire that his work be accessible to people from all cultures so that it might more effectively promote the unity of man.[22] Thus Stapledon deliberately avoided grounding his work in the daily experience of life in the Wirral, although he recognized that there was value in literary realism; he eschewed difficult and arcane literary allusions like those found in T. S. Eliot's *The Waste Land* and Joyce's *Ulysses*; and he preferred a direct, lucid style that would pose few problems for a translator. Above all, Stapledon has little affinity with the sort of writer Eliot was describing when he said of Henry James that he had "a mind so fine that no idea could violate it."[23] For Stapledon, the ideas always came first.

There is a temptation, in a study of this sort, to make extravagant claims for the writer under consideration, such as Richard Lupoff's assertion that Edgar Rice Burroughs will probably be recognized some day as one of the great American writers of the early twentieth century.[24] Even so, I feel safe in agreeing with Robert Scholes's description of Stapledon as "one of the great neglected authors of modern British fiction" and as "an important figure in the literary history of this century."[25] In the range of his vision, the universality and importance of his theme, the originality of his literary form, and the sustained elegance of his language, Stapledon has few peers. Small wonder, then, that there is a "boom" in studies of Stapledon's work: John Kinnaird's forthcoming monograph on Stapledon, the promise of a book-length study of Stapledon's novels by Leslie Fiedler, and the preparation of a Stapledon bibliography by Harvey Satty and Curtis Smith are all signs of the growing interest in Stapledon's fiction. There is also a need for the kind of "hard facts" scholarship that grows up around all major writers. A Stapledon biography and an edition of his letters would be of great value for those concerned with Stapledon's relation to other writers and thinkers of his time; the manuscripts located in Stapledon's library at "Simon's Field," along with others deposited at the University of Liverpool's Sydney Jones Library, may provide important clues about the process through which Stapledon conceived and developed his fictions; an edition of Stapledon's uncollected poems, arranged in chronological order, would help critics trace the development of Stapledon's ideas in the sixteen years between *Latter-Day Psalms* and *Last and First Men*.

Thirty years after Olaf Stapledon's death, serious study of his works is just beginning. There is no way of knowing what the outcome of that study will be, what the critical consensus will be a hundred years hence. There is, however, one indication that Stapledon's works have the power, the depth of expression, and the formal beauty needed to sustain interest in them across the generations: a second reading of virtually any work by Stapledon reveals a better work than it appeared to be the first time around, and the third reading reinforces the impression of the second. Like Stapledon himself, and like many of his characters, the novels often develop slowly, but their great staying power makes it seem probable that in years to come, more and more readers will turn to the pages of Stapledon's books for a confrontation with the crisis of the human spirit as seen through the lens of one man's agnostic mysticism.

Notes and References

Chapter One

1. Cited by Naomi Mitchison in *An Outline for Boys & Girls and Their Parents* (London: Victor Gollancz, 1932), p. 693. My major sources of biographical information in this chapter are my correspondence with Agnes Z. Stapledon and Harvey J. Satty; interviews with Agnes Z. Stapledon in Caldy, 20–21 June 1979; Sam Moskowitz, *Explorers of the Infinite* (Cleveland, 1963), pp. 261–77; and Moskowitz, "Olaf Stapledon: The Man Behind the Works," *Fantasy Commentator* 4 (Winter 1978–1979): 3–26, 32–33. Other sources are cited in the notes.

2. William Clibbett Stapledon and Reginald George Stapledon had the same father; they had different mothers, but their mothers were sisters. Thus the half-brothers were also first cousins.

3. *Youth and Tomorrow* (London, 1946), p. 7

4. Ibid., p. 41.

5. Moskowitz, "Olaf Stapledon: The Man Behind the Works," pp. 5–6. It is worth noting that *Ruskin's Guild of St. George* by Edith Hope Scott (London: Methuen, 1931) is dedicated to Emmeline Stapledon.

6. *Latter-Day Psalms* (Liverpool, 1914).

7. *Last Men in London* (London: Magnum Books, 1978), pp. 155–60.

8. "Experiences in the Friends' Ambulance Unit," in *We Did Not Fight 1914–18: Experiences of War Resisters,* ed. Julian Bell (London, 1935), pp. 359–74.

9. *Waking World* (London, 1934), p. 11.

10. Cosmopolis, the third title of a group known previously as the H. G. Wells Society and then as the Open Conspiracy, is mentioned by Saul Bellow in *Mr. Sammler's Planet:* "Included, for instance, with Gerald Heard and Olaf Stapledon in the *Cosmopolis* project for a World State, Sammler had written articles for *News of Progress,* for the other publication, *The World Citizen.* . . . Sammler, with growing interest and confidence recalling all this, lectured on *Cosmopolis* for half an hour, recalling what a kindhearted, ingenuous, stupid scheme it had been" (*Mr. Sammler's Planet* [New York: Penguin Books, 1977], p. 41). More detailed information about Cosmopolis

and related organizations can be found in W. Warren Wagar's *H. G. Wells and the World State* (New Haven: Yale University Press, 1961).

11. "Red Visitors Cause Rumpus," *Life*, 4 April 1949, pp. 39–43. The best account of Stapledon's participation in the meeting is given by Sam Moskowitz in "Peace and Olaf Stapledon," *Fantasy Commentator* 4 (Winter 1979–1980): 72–81. Stapledon's speeches at the conference are printed in *Speaking of Peace*, ed. Daniel S. Gillmor (New York, 1949).

12. Moskowitz, *Explorers of the Infinite*, p. 276, and "Olaf Stapledon: The Man behind the Works," p. 25.

13. "What *Are* 'Spiritual' Values?" in *Freedom of Expression: A Symposium*, ed. Herman Ould (London, 1944), p. 19.

14. *Saints and Revolutionaries* (London, 1939), p. 11.

15. Ibid., p. 7.

16. *New Hope for Britain* (London, 1939), p. 2.

17. Walter H. Gillings, "The Philosopher of Fantasy," *Scientifiction* 1, no.3 (June 1937): 9.

18. Letter to H. G. Wells dated 16 October 1931, H. G. Wells Collection, University of Illinois Library at Urbana–Champaign.

19. Patrick Parrinder, "Science Fiction and the Scientific World-View," in *Science Fiction: A Critical Guide*, ed. Parrinder (London: Longman, 1979), p. 69.

20. Curtis C. Smith makes a similar observation when he remarks that in *The Time Machine* "it's just barely possible to look at Eloi vs. Morlocks as good guys vs. BEM's, rather than as capitalists vs. proletarians. . . . By contrast, there are no potential BEM's in Stapledon's works, and no movies to be made starring Rod Taylor and Yvette Mimieux" ("Olaf Stapledon's Dispassionate Objectivity," in *Voices for the Future*, ed. Thomas D. Clareson [Bowling Green, Ohio, 1976], (pp. 44–45).

Chapter Two

1. Gillings, p. 8.

2. "The Last Judgment" was published in the English edition of *Possible Worlds and Other Papers* (1927; reprint ed., London: Chatto and Windus, 1945), pp. 287–312. "Man's Destiny" appeared in the American edition of the same book (New York: Harper & Brothers, 1928), pp. 300–305. Haldane's influence may also be seen in Stapledon's article "The Remaking of Man," *The Listener*, 8 April 1931; reprinted in *Fantasy Commentator* 4 (Winter 1978–1979): 27–29.

3. "Man's Destiny," p. 304.

4. Sam Moskowitz, *Strange Horizons: The Spectrum of Science Fiction*

(New York: Charles Scribner's Sons, 1976), p. 8; cf. his "Olaf Stapledon: The Man Behind the Works," p. 12.

5. "The Last Judgment," p. 312.

6. *Last and First Men* (London: Magnum Books, 1978). Parenthetical page references are to this edition.

7. Robert Scholes, *Structural Fabulation: An Essay on Fiction of the Future* (Notre Dame, Ind., 1975), p. 20.

8. See *Waking World,* pp. 10–13.

9. In the passage just cited, the monkeys' habit of covering their genitalia with metal may be a Swiftian reference, since it recalls Gulliver's unwillingness to reveal his private parts. The point here is that the monkeys illustrate various forms of corrupt or irrational behavior (like the Yahoos) in contrast to their Houyhnhnm-like role as rulers over debased species of mankind.

10. Smith, p. 48.

11. *Far Future Calling: A Radio Play* (New York, 1978), p. 10.

12. *Last Men in London* (London: Magnum Books, 1978). Parenthetical page references are to this edition.

13. C. M. Kornbluth, "The Failure of the Science Fiction Novel as Social Criticism," in *The Science Fiction Novel: Imagination and Social Criticism* (Chicago: Advent, 1969), p. 65.

14. This interpretation is supported by Stapledon's reference, in *Saints and Revolutionaries,* to our "half-born progressive culture" (p. 8).

15. Nietzsche, *Thus Spoke Zarathustra,* trans. R. J. Hollingdale (Baltimore: Penguin Books, 1969), pp. 41–42:

What is the ape to men? A laughing-stock or a painful embarrassment. And just so shall man be to the Superman: a laughing-stock or a painful embarrassment.

You have made your way from worm to man, and much in you is still worm. Once you were apes, and even now man is more of an ape than any ape.

Chapter Three

1. Janko Lavrin, *Nietzsche: A Biographical Introduction* (New York: Charles Scribner's Sons, 1971), p. 89.

2. *Thus Spoke Zarathustra,* pp. 43–44.

3. Harold Bloom, afterword to *Frankenstein* (New York: Signet, 1965), p. 215. It is worth noting that the treatment of the monster as a superior being disappears in the many Frankenstein movies, where the monster is almost invariably portrayed as slow-moving, inarticulate, dull-witted (or criminally insane), and childish.

4. Patrick Bridgwater has noted that G. K. Chesterton called *The Food of the Gods* "in essence a study of the [Nietzschean] Superman idea."

Bridgwater adds that the idea appears even earlier in Wells's fiction: in *The Island of Dr. Moreau* the title character is a demented version of the Nietzschean superman, while in *When the Sleeper Wakes* there is "what appears to be a straight echo of Nietzsche's doctrine of the Superman" (*Nietzsche in Anglosaxony* [Leicester: Leicester University Press, 1972], pp. 57–58).

5. Robert Scholes and Eric S. Rabkin, *Science Fiction: History-Science-Vision* (New York, 1977), p. 57.

6. Philip Wylie, *Gladiator* (1930; reprint ed., New York: Shakespeare House, 1951), p. 151.

7. J. D. Beresford, *The Hampdenshire Wonder* (1911; reprint ed., New York: Garland, 1975).

8. *Odd John* and *Sirius*, 1 vol. ed. (New York: Dover, 1972). Parenthetical page references for both books are to this edition.

9. Isaac Asimov, "Social Science Fiction," in *Turning Points: Essays on the Art of Science Fiction*, ed. Damon Knight (New York: Harper & Row, 1977), p. 46.

10. The destruction of the island where the utopian colony flourished is reminiscent of Jules Verne's *The Mysterious Island*. But Verne's story ends on a very different note from Stapledon's, for the inhabitants of Lincoln Island are rescued and taken to America, where they recreate their colony. Perhaps more to the point, the mass suicide in *Odd John* recalls the self-destruction of the Flying Men in *Last and First Men* as well as Humpty's death in *Last Men in London,* and anticipates Victor's suicide in *A Man Divided.*

11. Roger Brunet, "The Mystic Vision of Olaf Stapledon: The Spirit in Crisis" (M.A. thesis, Carleton University [Ottawa], 1968), p. 102.

12. Ibid., pp. 87–88.

13. "Education for Personality-in-Community," *New Era in Home and School* 27, no. 3 (March 1946): 66.

14. Brian Aldiss, *Billion Year Spree* (Garden City, N.Y.: Doubleday, 1973), p. 207.

15. H. H. Munro, *The Short Stories of Saki* (New York: Modern Library, 1958), pp. 119–26.

16. *Frankenstein,* p. 124. Elsewhere the creature complains to Frankenstein, "Remember that I am thy creature; I ought to be thy Adam, but I am rather the fallen angel, whom thou drivest from joy for no misdeed" (p. 95).

17. Ibid., p. 209; cf. *Paradise Lost,* IV, 110.

18. On a small scale this relationship recalls the pairings of Ichthyoids and Arachnoids, and the entire theme of symbiosis, in *Star Maker.*

19. Brunet, p. 128.

20. William L. Shirer, *The Rise and Fall of the Third Reich* (New York: Fawcett Publications, 1962), pp. 146–47.

21. Ibid., pp. 161–62.

22. Moskowitz, *Explorers of the Infinite,* pp. 267–68.

23. Barbara Bengels, "Olaf Stapledon's 'Odd John' and 'Sirius': Ascent into Bestiality," *Foundation* 9 (November 1975): 61.

Chapter Four

1. Aldiss, p. 208.

2. *Star Maker* (Harmondsworth, Middlesex: Penguin Books, 1972). Parenthetical page references are to this edition.

3. Scholes, p. 64.

4. This idea is very like the plot of Stanislaw Lem's satiric novel *The Futurological Congress* (1971), in which a government uses hallucinogenic drugs to create the illusion of utopian life while actual conditions become progressively more wretched.

5. This pattern also anticipates the plot of Isaac Asimov's classic science fiction story "Nightfall" (1941). That story takes place on a planet that receives light from six suns. Only once every two thousand years is there total darkness; when that happens, people go mad and burn their cities in an attempt to restore light. By the time daylight reappears, the civilization has been totally destroyed and must be rebuilt from scratch.

6. The interpretation of this section as an allusion to the rise of fascism may be substantiated by reference to Stapledon's description of the fascist mentality in *Waking World,* p. 6: "Revolting against commercialism, [fascists] praise martial and barbaric virtues, the tribal spirit, and the fictitious entity which they call 'the race'. Sickened by the ineffectiveness of so-called democracy, they crave a dictator . . . [who] encourages the most flagrant hooliganism and sadism on the part of the horde of muddle-headed young men whom he uses to enforce his will."

7. *Waking World,* p. 3.

8. Smith, p. 52.

9. In *Pudd'nhead Wilson* (1894), a light-skinned Negro slave substitutes her even lighter baby boy for the infant son of her master. Brought up thinking he is white, her son becomes an arrogant, selfish, and irresponsible master, while the real master's son, who is treated as a slave, becomes the stereotypical "darkie." The substitution is at last discovered by the title character, who among other things is an expert on fingerprints.

10. Alexander Pope, *An Essay on Man,* I, 294.

11. Brunet, p. 47.

12. Brunet, Abstract.

13. Albert Camus, *The Stranger,* trans. Stuart Gilbert (New York: Vintage Books, 1946), p. 154.

14. *Nebula Maker,* ed. Harvey Satty (London: Sphere Books, 1979). Parenthetical page references are to this edition, and I have used the form of the title given in this paperback edition rather than that of the original edition: *"Nebula maker"* (Hayes, Middlesex, 1976).

15. *Saints and Revolutionaries,* p. 18.

16. Ibid., p. 60.

Chapter Five

1. *Waking World,* pp. 105–6.

2. *Darkness and the Light* (1942; reprint ed. Westport, Conn.: Hyperion Press, 1974). Parenthetical page references are to this edition.

3. "A Note on Magnitude" appended to *Star Maker.*

4. E. W. Martin, "Between the Devil and the Deep Sea: The Philosophy of Olaf Stapledon," in *The Pleasure Ground,* ed. Malcolm Elwin (London, 1947), p. 214.

5. *Worlds of Wonder: Three Tales of Fantasy* (Los Angeles: Fantasy Publishing Co., 1949) contains *The Flames, Death into Life,* and *Old Man in New World.* Parenthetical page references for these three works are to this edition.

6. It is worth noting that *Sirius,* which is Stapledon's finest study of a character "caught between two worlds," was also published in 1944.

7. Fletcher Pratt, "Science Fiction & Fantasy—1949," *Saturday Review of Literature,* 24 December 1949, p. 23. Appropriate as it might have been with respect to *Death into Life,* Pratt's comment was actually aimed at the entire *Worlds of Wonder* volume—including *The Flames,* which certainly does not lack drive and interest.

8. Edwin A. Abbott, *Flatland: A Romance of Many Dimensions* (New York: Barnes & Noble, 1963). Stapledon refers to Abbott's satire in *Last Men in London,* p. 198.

9. Sam Moskowitz, *"The Flames: A Fantasy,"* *Fantasy Commentator,* 2 (Winter 1947–1948): 158.

Chapter Six

1. Bloom, p. 213.

2. See Corbett H. Thigpen and Hervey M. Cleckley, *The Three Faces of Eve* (Kingsport, Tenn.: Kingsport Press, 1957); Evelyn Lancaster (pseud.),

The Final Face of Eve (New York: McGraw-Hill, 1958); and Flora Rheta Schreiber, *Sybil* (Chicago: Henry Regnery, 1973). Although these widely known cases appeared after Stapledon's book, there was already a well-developed list of major studies of multiple personality by the time *A Man Divided* was composed. For a survey of cases of multiple personality, discussion of theories, and a bibliography of studies, see W. S. Taylor and Mabel F. Martin, "Multiple Personality," *Journal of Abnormal and Social Psychology* 39 (1944): 281–300. Stapledon owned a copy of the 1919 reprinting of one of the books listed by Taylor and Martin: Boris Sidis and Simon P. Goodhart, *Multiple Personality* (New York: D. Appleton, 1904).

    3. *A Man Divided* (London, 1950). Parethetical page references are to this edition.

    4. *Youth and Tomorrow*, pp. 106–7.

    5. Moskowitz, *Explorers of the Infinite*, p. 276.

    6. Personal interview with Agnes Z. Stapledon, 20–21 June 1979. When I asked Mrs. Stapledon to explain the dedication to *A Man Divided* ("To A in gratitude to her for being T"), she said *A* was her real name, Agnes, and *T* was Taffy, a pet name taken from Rudyard Kipling's *Just So Stories*. In "How the First Letter Was Written," "How the Alphabet Was Made," and "The Tabu Tale," Taffy is portrayed as a lovable, playful, slightly mischievous girl—just the opposite of the sort of person implied by an "old-fashioned" name like Agnes.

    7. Mrs. Stapledon made the suggestion that Pax's character is based on hers (interview, 20–21 June 1979).

    8. Moskowitz, "Olaf Stapledon: The Man Behind the Works," p. 26.

    9. *Beyond the "Isms"* (London, 1942), pp. 52–56.

    10. *Waking World*, pp. 244–52.

    11. *The Opening of the Eyes*, ed. Agnes Z. Stapledon (London, 1954). Parenthetical references to the book and its preface are to this edition.

    12. Moskowitz, *Explorers of the Infinite*, p. 277.

    13. Moskowitz, "Olaf Stapledon: The Man Behind the Works," p. 26.

    14. Cf. *Saints and Revolutionaries*, p. 100.

    15. Personal correspondence from Agnes Z. Stapledon, 13 September 1979.

    16. *4 Encounters* (Hayes, Middlesex, 1976). Parenthetical page references are to this edition; quotations have been checked against a photostatic copy of Stapledon's typescript.

    17. *The Poetry and Prose of William Blake*, ed. David V. Erdman (Garden City, N.Y.: Doubleday, 1970), p. 35.

    18. For other references to the death of Lenin's brother, see *Death into*

Life (in *Worlds of Wonder*, p. 172), *Beyond the "Isms,"* p. 50, and *Odd John* (*Odd John* and *Sirius*, p. 61).

19. *The Collected Poems of W. B. Yeats* (New York: Macmillan, 1976), p. 336.

20. The stories are printed, along with *Far Future Calling*, Stapledon's essay "Interplanetary Man?" and two articles by Sam Moskowitz, in *Far Future Calling: Uncollected Science Fiction and Fantasies of Olaf Stapledon*, ed. Sam Moskowitz (Philadelphia, 1979).

Chapter Seven

1. Basil Davenport, "The Vision of Olaf Stapledon," introduction to *To the End of Time: The Best of Olaf Stapledon* (New York, 1953), p. vii.

2. Doris Lessing, *Re: Colonised Planet 5, Shikasta* (New York: Alfred A. Knopf, 1979), p. x.

3. Lessing, p. 40.

4. Cited by Roger Lancelyn Green and Walter Hooper in *C. S. Lewis: A Biography* (New York: Harcourt Brace Jovanovich, 1974), p. 163.

5. *Letters of C. S. Lewis,* ed. W. H. Lewis (New York: Harcourt, Brace & World, 1966), p. 160.

6. Green and Hooper, p. 173.

7. C. S. Lewis, "On Science Fiction," in *Of Other Worlds: Essays and Stories,* ed. Walter Hooper (New York: Harcourt, Brace & World, 1966), p. 66.

8. C. S. Lewis, *That Hideous Strength* (New York: Macmillan Paperbacks Edition, 1965), p. 7.

9. C. S. Lewis, *Perelandra* (New York: Macmillan Paperbacks Edition, 1965), pp. 81–82.

10. C. S. Lewis, *Out of the Silent Planet* (New York: Macmillan Paperbacks Edition, 1965), pp. 135–36.

11. Scholes and Rabkin, p. 46.

12. Green and Hooper, p. 178.

13. Arthur C. Clarke, introduction to *The Lion of Comarre & Against the Fall of Night* (New York: Harcourt, Brace & World, 1968), p. vii.

14. Discussion following Olaf Stapledon, "Interplanetary Man?" *Journal of the British Interplanetary Society* 7 (November 1948): 232.

15. Quoted by Eric S. Rabkin in *Arthur C. Clarke* (West Linn, Ore.: Stormont House, 1979), p. 10.

16. Arthur C. Clarke, *Profiles of the Future* (New York: Harper & Row, 1962), p. 185.

17. Arthur C. Clarke, *Childhood's End* (New York: Ballantine Books, 1975), p. 206.

18. Peter Brigg, "The Three Styles of Arthur C. Clarke: The Projector, the Wit, and the Mystic," in *Arthur C. Clarke,* ed. Joseph D. Olander and Martin Harry Greenberg (New York: Taplinger, 1977), p. 42.

19. Cited by Darko Suvin in "The Open-Ended Parables of Stanislaw Lem and *Solaris,*" afterword to *Solaris,* trans. Joanna Kilmartin and Steve Cox (New York: Berkley Medallion Books, 1971), p. 223.

20. *Solaris,* p. 180.

21. Ezra Pound, *ABC of Reading* (London: George Routledge, 1934), p. 23.

22. See Stapledon's "Literature and the Unity of Man," in *Writers in Freedom: A Symposium,* ed. Herman Ould (London, 1942), pp. 113–19.

23. Quoted by Maurice Beebe in "*Ulysses* and the Age of Modernism," *James Joyce Quarterly* 10 (Fall 1972): 179.

24. Richard A. Lupoff, *Edgar Rice Burroughs: Master of Adventure,* rev. ed. (New York: Ace Books, 1968), p. 33.

25. Scholes, pp. 19, 21.

Bibliography

PRIMARY SOURCES

1. Books

Latter-Day Psalms. Liverpool: Henry Young & Sons, 1914.

A Modern Theory of Ethics: A Study of the Relations of Ethics and Psychology. London: Methuen, 1929.

Last and First Men: A Story of the Near and Far Future. London: Methuen, 1930.

Last Men in London. London: Methuen, 1932.

Waking World. London: Methuen, 1934.

Odd John: A Story Between Jest and Earnest. London: Methuen, 1935.

Star Maker. London: Methuen, 1937.

Saints and Revolutionaries. London: William Heinemann, 1939.

New Hope for Britain. London: Methuen, 1939.

Philosophy and Living. 2 vols. Harmondsworth, Middlesex: Penguin, 1939.

Darkness and the Light. London: Methuen, 1942.

Beyond the "Isms." London: Secker & Warburg, Searchlight Books, no. 16, 1942.

Old Man in New World. London: Allen and Unwin, 1944.

Sirius: A Fantasy of Love and Discord. London: Secker & Warburg, 1944.

Seven Pillars of Peace. London: Common Wealth, 1944.

Death into Life. London: Methuen, 1946.

Youth and Tomorrow. London: St. Botolph, 1946.

The Flames: A Fantasy. London: Secker & Warburg, 1947.

A Man Divided. London: Methuen, 1950.

The Opening of the Eyes. Edited by Agnes Z. Stapledon. London: Methuen, 1954.

4 Encounters. Hayes, Middlesex: Bran's Head Books, 1976.

"Nebula maker." Hayes, Middlesex: Bran's Head Books, 1976.

Far Future Calling: A Radio Play. Edited by Harvey Satty. New York: S Press, Olaf Stapledon Society, 1978.

Far Future Calling: Uncollected Science Fiction and Fantasies of Olaf

Stapledon. Edited by Sam Moskowitz. Philadelphia: Oswald Train, 1979.

2. Selected Articles

"The Remaking of Man." *The Listener* 5 (8 April 1931): 575–76. Reprinted in *Fantasy Commentator* 4 (Winter 1978–1979): 27–29.

"Problems and Solutions, or the Future." In *An Outline for Boys & Girls and Their Parents,* edited by Naomi Mitchison. London: Victor Gollancz, 1932. Pp. 691–749.

"Education and World Citizenship." In *Manifesto: Being the Book of the Federation of Progressive Societies and Individuals,* edited by C. E. M. Joad. London: George Allen & Unwin, 1934. Pp. 142–63.

"Experiences in the Friends' Ambulance Unit." In *We Did Not Fight 1914–18: Experiences of War Resisters,* edited by Julian Bell. London: Cobden-Sanderson, 1935. Pp. 359–74.

"Literature and the Unity of Man." In *Writers in Freedom: A Symposium,* edited by Herman Ould. London: Hutchinson, [1942]. Pp. 113–19.

"What *Are* 'Spiritual' Values?" In *Freedom of Expression: A Symposium,* edited by Herman Ould. London: Hutchinson, 1944. Pp. 16–26.

"Man: Should We Re-Make Him?" *Leader* 2 (1 September 1945): 12–13.

"Education for Personality-in-Community." *New Era in Home and School* 27, no. 3 (March 1946): 63–67.

"Data for a World View: 1. The Human Situation and Natural Science." *Enquiry* 1, no. 1 (April 1948): 13–18.

"Data for a World View: 2. Paranormal Experiences." *Enquiry* 1, no. 2 (May 1948): 13–18.

"Interplanetary Man?" *Journal of the British Interplanetary Society* 7 (November 1948): 213–33.

"Ethical Values Common to East and West" and "From England." In *Speaking of Peace,* edited by Daniel Gillmor. New York: National Council of the Arts, Sciences and Professions, 1949. Pp. 119–21, 130–31.

"Personality and Living." *Philosophy* 24 (April 1949): 144–56.

"The Bridge Between [Marxist Values and Christian Values]." In *Two Worlds in Focus: Studies of the Cold War.* London: National Peace Council, 1950. Pp. 44–60.

"The Ways of Peace." *One World* 3 (October–November 1950): 178–85.

SECONDARY SOURCES

ALDISS, BRIAN W. *Billion Year Spree: The True History of Science Fiction.* Garden City, N.Y.: Doubleday, 1973. This useful general survey of science fiction helps to place Stapledon's novels within the context of their genre.

BAILEY, K. V. "A Prized Harmony: Myth, Symbol and Dialectic in the Novels of Olaf Stapledon." *Foundation* 15 (January 1979): 53–66. In his study of Stapledon's mythmaking, Bailey argues that the power of the novels derives from "Stapledon's ability to shape, from the large problems of human ethics, cosmic dramas shot through with overtones of myth; and, in doing this, to give novel form and imagery to certain universal archetypes."

BENGELS, BARBARA. "Olaf Stapledon's 'Odd John' and 'Sirius': Ascent into Bestiality." *Foundation* 9 (November 1975): 57–61. Finding "a greater richness and vitality" in *Sirius* than in *Odd John,* Bengels contends that readers find "a kindred humanity" in Sirius but not in the superhuman John.

BRUNET, ROGER ANDREW. "The Mystic Vision of Olaf Stapledon: The Spirit in Crisis." M. A. thesis, Carleton University (Ottawa), 1968. This study of four major novels—*Star Maker, Last and First Men, Odd John,* and *Sirius*—is a sophisticated analysis of the ways Stapledon deals with the concept of "spirit."

COATES, J. B. *Ten Modern Prophets.* London: Frederick Muller, 1944. The ninth chapter (pp. 151–66) summarizes and occasionally criticizes the dominant themes of Stapledon's social philosophy.

DAVENPORT, BASIL. "The Vision of Olaf Stapledon." Introduction to *To The End of Time: The Best of Olaf Stapledon.* 1953. Reprint. Boston: G. K. Hall, 1975. Pp. vii–xiv. This is a brief but useful introduction to Stapledon's themes.

ELKINS, CHARLES. "The Worlds of Olaf Stapledon: Myth or Fiction?" *Mosaic* 13 (Spring / Summer 1980): 145–52. Elkins contends "that: a) Stapledon is not creating myth, and b) to the extent that he tries, his works violate some of the very assumptions upon which science fiction rests."

FIEDLER, LESLIE. Introduction to *Odd John.* London: New English Library, 1978. Pp. 7–13. This essay is stimulating, but it contains too many errors to be considered reliable as a guide to Stapledon's life and art.

GILLINGS, WALTER H. "Olaf Stapledon's Fantasy on the Men of the

Space Age: What Shall We Do with the Planets?" *Fantasy Review*, December 1948, pp. 10–12. Gillings summarizes Stapledon's October 1948 lecture to the British Interplanetary Society.

————. "The Philosopher of Fantasy: How Dr. Olaf Stapledon Discovered Science Fiction Magazines." *Scientifiction: The British Fantasy Review* 1, no. 3 (June 1937): 8–10. This account of an interview with Stapledon includes information about the origins of *Last and First Men* and about Stapledon's attitudes toward science fiction and science.

GLICKSOHN, SUSAN. "A City of Which the Stars Are Suburbs." In *SF: The Other Side of Realism,* edited by Thomas D. Clareson. Bowling Green, Ohio: Bowling Green University Popular Press, 1971. Pp. 334–47. Glicksohn compares the uses of mythic histories in *Last and First Men* and Isaac Asimov's *Foundation Trilogy.*

LAVABRE, SIMONE. "Un utopiste au XXe siècle, W. Olaf Stapledon." *Caliban* 3, no. 2 (1967): 249–66. The author analyzes Stapledon's treatment of scientific ideas in *Last and First Men* and *The Flames.*

MARTIN, E. W. "Between the Devil and the Deep Sea: The Philosophy of Olaf Stapledon." In *The Pleasure Ground: A Miscellany of English Writing,* edited by Malcolm Elwin. London: MacDonald, 1947. Pp. 204–16. Martin outlines Stapledon's philosophical argument and distinguishes Stapledon's ideas from those of his contemporaries.

MICHEL, JOHN B. "The Philosophical Novels of Olaf Stapledon: Studies in a New Type of Outlook." *The Alchemist,* Summer 1940, pp. 7–15. Michel, a Marxist critic of science fiction, regards Stapledon as "the last truly great bourgeois philosopher, the first exponent of a cosmical philosophy and the sorely needed link between the materialist Marxian Smeltanschuung and the unknown future."

MOSKOWITZ, SAM. *Explorers of the Infinite: Shapers of Science Fiction.* Cleveland: World, 1963. Despite some errors, the chapter entitled "Olaf Stapledon: Cosmic Philosopher" (also available as the introduction to the Hyperion Press reprint of *Darkness and the Light*) is a good general survey of Stapledon's life and the themes of his books.

————. "Olaf Stapledon: The Man Behind the Works." *Fantasy Commentator* 4 (Winter 1978–1979): 3–26, 32–33. Based partly on interviews with Stapledon's family and friends, this is the most detailed biographical article yet written about Stapledon. Along with "Peace and Olaf Stapledon," this essay is reprinted in Moskowitz's edition of *Far Future Calling: The Uncollected Science Fiction and Fantasies of Olaf Stapledon.*

————. "Peace and Olaf Stapledon," *Fantasy Commentator* 4 (Winter 1979–1980): 72–81. A briefer version of this account of Stapledon's participation in the Cultural and Scientific Conference for Peace in March 1949 appeared under the title "Bold Man in New World," in *Shangri-La,* no. 14 (October 1949): pp. 5–8.

SCHOLES, ROBERT. *Structural Fabulation: An Essay on Fiction of the Future.* Notre Dame, Ind.: University of Notre Dame Press, 1975. Scholes calls Stapledon "one of the great neglected authors of modern British fiction" and comments on structure and vision in *Star Maker.*

SCHOLES, ROBERT, and ERIC S. RABKIN. *Science Fiction: History-Science-Vision.* New York: Oxford University Press, 1977. In addition to passing references to Stapledon's works there is an analysis of *Star Maker* as one of ten "representative" science fiction novels.

SMITH, CURTIS C. "The Books of Olaf Stapledon: A Chronological Survey." *Science-Fiction Studies* 1 (Fall 1974): 297–99. Smith provides full bibliographical information and a summary of the main ideas of each of Stapledon's books through *The Opening of the Eyes.*

———. "Olaf Stapledon: Saint and Revolutionary." *Extrapolation* 13 (1971): 5–15. Focusing primarily on *Last and First Men,* the author tries to show that "Stapledon is a revolutionary prophet, synthesizing all knowledge until it becomes useful and comprehensible and can help man to extend his nature to new levels of perception."

———. "Olaf Stapledon's Dispassionate Objectivity." In *Voices for the Future: Essays on Major Science Fiction Writers,* edited by Thomas D. Clareson. Bowling Green, Ohio: Bowling Green University Popular Press, 1976. Pp. 44–63. This analysis of *Last and First Men, Star Maker, Odd John,* and *Sirius* demonstrates their concern with the dialectic of matter and intelligence and considers their political, social, and ethical implications.

Index